Exercising Your Ethics

Through a witty and engaging style the author invites readers to consider their character authenticity at work. The book is for people who want to do the right thing, but may not be sure what that means, how to go about it, or how to withstand the forces that may push them away from wanting to be ethical. In a world that seems to reward winning, regardless of how it is achieved, we need a clearer reason for wanting to be and become our best selves. Poking fun at the ironies and hypocrisies of human behavior, *Exercising Your Ethics* prompts you to leverage techniques that will help you become more deliberate about choosing value-driven actions.

Exercising Your Ethics explains the messy business of workplace ethics in a way that is relatable and relevant. Readers will learn to build moral strength and encourage its development in others, while also recognizing moral vulnerability traps. It is an ideal resource for adult business education and training in academic or organizational settings. Educators, HR professionals, team leaders, coaches, and trainers will find this book a guide for competency development and as a way to prompt reflective discourse.

Illustrator **Ralph Underhill** produces cartoons for a diverse number of social and environmental movements. He has a particular interest in using artistic communications to motivate positive change.

Leslie E. Sekerka takes a uniquely proactive approach to her teaching and scholarship. She is a Professor Emeritus of Business Ethics and founding Director of the *Ethics in Action Center* at Menlo College, located in Silicon Valley. Her interest in adult moral development stems from her work in business, the military, and academia, intertwining practice and empirical research to create effective management education. Her books on moral development include *Ethics Is a Daily Deal* for adult learners and the *Being a Better Bear* book series for children. She works with business and government leaders on emerging ethical issues, helping to create and sustain organizational ethical cultures that build and sustain moral strength.

Exercising Your Ethics
Bringing Moral Strength to Business

Leslie E. Sekerka

Routledge
Taylor & Francis Group

LONDON AND NEW YORK

First published 2022
by Routledge
2 Park Square, Milton Park, Abingdon, Oxon OX14 4RN

and by Routledge
605 Third Avenue, New York, NY 10158

Routledge is an imprint of the Taylor & Francis Group, an informa business

British Library Cataloguing-in-Publication Data
A catalogue record for this book is available from the British Library

Library of Congress Cataloging-in-Publication Data
Names: Sekerka, Leslie E, author.
Title: Exercising your ethics : bringing moral strength to business /
Leslie E Sekerka.
Description: First Edition. | New York : Routledge, 2022. |
Identifiers: LCCN 2021011823 (print) | LCCN 2021011824 (ebook) |
ISBN 9780367341763 (hardback) | ISBN 9781032009377 (paperback) |
ISBN 9780429324284 (ebook)
Subjects: LCSH: Business ethics. | Personnel management—Moral and
ethical aspects.
Classification: LCC HF5387 .S434 2022 (print) |
LCC HF5387 (ebook) | DDC 174/.4—dc23
LC record available at https://lccn.loc.gov/2021011823
LC ebook record available at https://lccn.loc.gov/2021011824

ISBN: 978-0-367-34176-3 (hbk)
ISBN: 978-1-032-00937-7 (pbk)
ISBN: 978-0-429-32428-4 (ebk)

DOI: 10.4324/9780429324284

Typeset in Georgia
by codeMantra

Contents

Introduction
Let the good times roll

Do you want to be successful by accomplishing your business goals without causing harm to other people and the planet?

Sure you do.

You're a good person.

It's not simple or easy, but it's possible!

To achieve the bottom line in an ethical way, your organization needs your attention and care. This requires maintaining a desire and commitment to exercising your values. Many people say they have a desire to be ethical, but they don't have a plan for how to sustain their convictions.

Ethics is a practice.

If you want to be good at something you need to do it routinely. This book highlights examples and exercises that are designed to help you build your moral

DOI: 10.4324/9780429324284-1

strength, and thereby fortify the ethics of your organization. Regardless of whatever field you're in—data analytics, manufacturing, human resources, marketing, customer service, finance, engineering, technology, or general management— you will be able to relate to the material presented. No matter what position you hold, *Exercising Your Ethics* offers insights that are practical and can be applied immediately.

The challenge with any organization, whether it's a startup or an established corporation, is that the drivers for success can simultaneously interrupt or block the desire to engage in ethical decision-making and moral action.

> *A myopic focus on success threatens your moral identity.*

> *When multiple people disregard their moral values, society reflects this and cascades degradation into the future.*

To explain this concern, I am writing as if you are here with me. If you decide to leave (quit reading), I urge you to at least take a peek at the cartoons before you go!

You may ask: Why are there cartoons in an ethics book?

Why not?

Ralph's artwork complements the stories, cases, and examples, which illustrate how some individuals and organizations have failed to uphold their values. You'll see how patterns of unethical behavior can lead to very serious consequences. The idea is to sustain your attention by sparking interest, curiosity, and introspection, encouraging you to be honest with yourself. Drawing from the latest research, you'll see how the ironies of our everyday actions contribute to character depletion and ethical corner cutting. There are specific activities you can participate in that will strengthen your moral competency to prevent moral decay. Taking a proactive approach to business ethics is intended to help you succeed by learning to defend and bolster your best self.

While business ethics is a serious subject, it's important not to take ourselves too seriously.

Humor and laughter are healthy for us![1]

It is also the elixir for many a human vice (including boredom).[2]

I also have a specific reason for wanting you to experience humor as you read. Laughter creates endorphins, which free up your mind for learning.[3] Cognition and emotion are not separate entities. They work together in an anatomical structure complemented by chemical processes. For effective learning, it's important to be in a feel-good frame of mind and have minimal stress.[4]

So I say: Let the good times roll!

I promise you this is an easy read. And I dare say, it's a lot more fun than your typical "ethics" textbook.

I should know, I wrote one of those![5]

To be clear, I assume that you are familiar with some of the cases and, very importantly, that you have a modicum of desire to do the right thing.

At least most of the time!

As it is for me, along with everyone else out there in business, it's important to learn how to flex your ethical muscles. Just because you want to do the right thing, doesn't mean you will always know what to do in a given situation. This book is designed to help you better understand how to go about addressing an ethical issue and to deal with the forces that might prohibit you from wanting to do so.

Let's step out of our everyday routines that can inadvertently drive our subtle automatic pilot way of going about business ethics. Take a deep dive into thinking about what we're doing and why we're doing it. I'll ask you to recall your motivations, drives, and weaknesses, identifying those that might allow you (or others) to ignore, trample over, or reject the desire to be ethical.

In a world that seems to reward immediacy and short-term thinking, with a rampant "winner-take-all" mindset and too many binary extremes, cultivating affirmations that support ethicality seem to be missing. We need encouragement to be our best selves and to demonstrate our moral identity. To do this, we need to perceive, understand, and execute the virtues that are within all of us.

*More specifically, the character strengths that reside within **you**!*

To help you do this, we'll examine your values, human nature, and insights about your own moral development. I'll leverage discoveries from prominent scholars in the fields of business ethics, sociology, positive psychology, management, and organizational behavior. You'll be exposed to intriguing stories about the following:

• Recognizing your fudge factor

- Rationalizing your worst and practicing your best self
- Accessing your moral emotions (guilt, shame, and pride)
- Self-regulation as your superpower
- Applying goal setting to motivate your moral strength
- Forming your own posse for ethical reporting

Taken together, the chapters will help you realize how an ethical approach will work out better for you (and your organization) in the long run.

This might seem obvious.

But it's not.

If it were, we wouldn't have so many ethical issues in business!

When we are faced with competing goals, morality being one of them, ethics often comes in second.

Sometimes last...or not at all!

Spare me the good apple, bad apple routine. Get my lawyer!

We need to practice making a concerted effort to engage in moral awareness and action, not just say or assume that we are doing so. To do this, we have to continually revisit, say hello to, and exercise our own moral identity continuously.

That means exercising the values you say you hold.

Business ethics is crucial, not just because it's morally "right," but because it makes sense. The advantages of exercising your ethics benefit the firm and also extend out into every area of your life, including your family and community. When corporate leaders shirk their social and environmental responsibilities, it makes our role as moral agents that much more challenging.

Bad apples are out there.

But remember, we are all stakeholders.

So everyone has the power to create change.

To move us in the direction of positive ethical development, I'll help you become aware of some of the natural human barriers that might inadvertently block you from being ethical in business. As my friend and colleague Dr Tom Plante at Santa Clara University says, "We need to think about who we want to be in the world."[6]

Ultimately this is your decision.

Let the ride begin!

Notes

1 Beard, A. (2014). Leading with humor. *Harvard Business Review*, 92(5), 130–131. Downloaded from: https://hbr.org/2014/05/leading-with-humor.
2 Heggie, Betty-Ann. (November 16, 2018). The benefits of laughing in the office. *Harvard Business Review*. Downloaded from: https://hbr.org/2018/11/the-benefits-of-laughing-in-the-office?referral=03759&cm_vc=rr_item_page.bottom.
3 *Healthline*. (May 1, 2020). What are endorphins? *Healthline*. Downloaded from: https://www.healthline.com/health/endorphins.
4 Schachl, H. (2016). Neuroscience: A traditional and innovative approach to education with focus on stress with learning. *Signum Temporis*, 8(1), 9.
5 Sekerka, L. E. (2016). *Ethics is a daily deal: Choosing to build moral strength as a practice*. Basel: Springer International Publishing AG.
6 Plante, T. G. (2004). *Do the right thing: Living ethically in an unethical world*. Oakland, CA: New Harbinger Publications (ISBN-13: 978-1572243644).

1 Business ethics *is* an oxymoron

This is not a question. It's simply a statement of fact.

Business ethics is like having an unbiased opinion, taking a working vacation, earning negative income, or acting natural. It has become an oxymoron, i.e., a phrase in which seemingly contradictory terms appear in conjunction.

For years I argued against this claim.

DOI: 10.4324/9780429324284-2

But recently, I have seen enough evidence that has turned this wordplay into a reality. When I meet people, regardless of the setting (social gatherings, community activities, or while traveling), they usually ask me:

What do you do?

Rather than asking about family or personal interests, Americans, in particular, tend to dive intently toward work-related conversations. Jobs or career choices might suggest certain lifestyles. They are also likely to reveal implicit biases. For example, minutes into an

initial dialogue, I'm invariably asked about the details of my profession.

The Conversation Goes Like This...

So, what do you do?

I'm a teacher.

Oh really, what grade?

I teach big kids, adults.

So, you're a professor?

Yes.

What do you teach?

Business ethics.

As soon as I say, "business ethics," now it gets interesting.

Check out the change in how people have reacted to that statement over the past two decades:

1990...Tell me more. What's that about?

1995...Oh yeah, I've heard about that.

2000...Really, how interesting!

2005...That's so important. We should do more.

2010...Isn't that all over the news right now?

2015...You have a lot to keep you busy; great job security!

2020...Is there such a thing?

I fear the future reaction will be:

2025...Who cares?

If we're going to reverse this trend, it comes down to the fact that ethics is a choice. Each of us must practice exercising the values we say we hold.

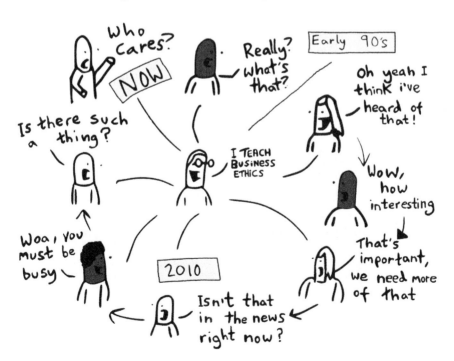

As a business ethicist, it pains me to openly admit that the overarching landscape of today's global economy does not celebrate this topic.

Business ethics is often a figure of speech, rather than a corporate reality. The two words appear in sequence but frequently contradict one another. It's almost as though they remain in separate galaxies, so far apart that it's hard to imagine where they comingle, much less complement one another.

I've come to the realization that an accurate portrayal of ethics in business is much like the backdrop or stage setting for a theatrical play. It's designed to look like something that may not be there.

Maybe it has always been this way.

Or, perhaps it is now more painfully obvious (in the twenty-first century) that the workplace has been shaped (either deliberately or as an unintended consequence) to ensure that other values (like money) supersede honesty, commitment, loyalty, fairness, transparency, and quality. In the race to disrupt, innovate, move faster, cut costs, connect globally, and be "smarter," we have reduced the value of ethics as a praiseworthy norm. We like the sound of "being ethical." But are we willing to do the work to make it genuine?

Certainly not enough!

Corporations may superficially claim to be ethical, backed by marketing, glossy brochures, and annual check-in-the-box training programs.

However, the backbone of many business operations lacks moral authenticity. Maybe an intention to be ethical was originally there. But when put to the test, how does the organization step up and embrace its stakeholders' concerns?

Consider Apple. They say they care about sustainability for people and the planet. And yet, their business model is hypocritical. They subtly promote built-in obsolescence by encouraging ongoing device replacement. In the case dubbed "batterygate," Apple agreed to pay $113 million to settle an investigation by nearly three dozen U.S. states. The firm's past practices slowed customers older models down. Their throttling efforts drew nationwide scorn, shocking their customer base who, at the time, saw this manipulation as an attempt to nudge them into buying new and more expensive products.[1] Encouraging replacement also increases environmental harms throughout the product's supply chain. One iPhone is said to produce approximately 79 kilograms of CO_2 emissions. In volume, 1 kilogram is about half a cubic meter, which equates to filling up two bathtubs.

Do the math and picture it.

That's roughly 158 bathtub-size "clouds" of CO_2 emissions created for every iPhone sold. In 2019, that number was 40.8 million (multiply that by 158).[2]

You get the idea.

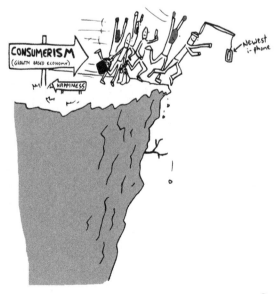

@CARTOONRALPH

Amplifying this concern is the fact that iPhones are fabricated with the use of conflict minerals. These are resources mined and sold in regions experiencing active conflict, where human rights violations and abuse occur in pursuit of valuable minerals.[3] While an environmentally sound iPhone was introduced, its price point is totally unaffordable to the average consumer ($1,450). The *Ethical Consumer* consistently rates Apple poorly in areas of environment sustainability and human rights.[4]

In addition to questionable stakeholder practices, Apple has relished its ability to control and market dominate. Called to task by the European Union (EU), the Commission has charged the company with monopolistic behavior, inappropriately forcing apps to use its in-app payment system. Additionally, Apple is charged with antitrust violations for allegedly abusing its control over the distribution of music-streaming apps, amplifying the existing U.S. federal lawsuit regarding Epic Games.[5]

The tech giant Google once stated boldly in its corporate Code of Conduct that the company would "do no evil."[6] After adhering to this commitment for nearly

two decades, it was retracted from their code one night without consulting with the employees. While a hint of this verbiage remains within the firm's documentation, it's interesting that the burden of the responsibility is now placed on organizational members, not the company itself. It reads:

> And remember...don't be evil, and if you see something that you think isn't right – speak up![7]

Over the past few years, Googlers have voiced their concerns about witnessing a shift in the company's "greed and abuse of power" since it pivoted away from a focus on serving the greater good.[8] Employee leaders who have since left the firm claim that the company now prioritizes profits over human rights.

Take heart

Don't give up! There are companies out there who are truly committed to being ethical. They're humble enough to realize they're not perfect, and they continue to work at "doing well and doing good." A clue on how to find them is to see how they go about achieving their goals. Instead of singing their praises, they're busy actively pursuing stakeholder capitalism.

Ethical decisions made by corporations include Best Buy's commitment to environmental sustainability, the move by CVS to stop selling tobacco products, a commitment to animal welfare by McDonald's and Chipotle Mexican Grill, with initiatives to produce "ethically-raised" meat, and Sony's focus on stakeholder safety.

The ethics of a company are only as sound as its last decisions and action, at the close of business that day.

Sometimes ethical business champions are found within smaller, privately held operations. Understanding how stated values are transferred into products and services can sometimes be easier to perceive in entrepreneurial startups. Their success may blossom and ultimately become a well-known brand. Companies like Patagonia, Ben & Jerry's, Seventh Generation, Earthbound Farm, Eileen Fisher, Danone, and Natura are worth examining for best practices.

Now it's your turn!

Take a moment to think about companies you like to do business with. Name three of them:

1. _____
2. _____
3. _____
_____

Why do you appreciate these companies?

Do these firms have integrity? How do you know?

How do these organizations treat people and the planet?

If you're interested in ethical excellence, companies that have a B Corp Certification provide a great starting point for role-modeling. Certified B Corporations are businesses that meet the highest standards of verified social and environmental performance, public transparency, and legal accountability to balance profit with purpose.[9] These companies are continually working to redefine success in business, through inclusivity and sustainability. B Corp organizations choose to influence society for good, as they make money.

Business has always influenced society. But society can also shape business as well. The intersection of business and society truly reflects our culture. As everyone around the world simultaneously experienced the global public health and economic crisis brought on by Covid-19, every aspect of life "as we knew it" was impacted. Our professional and personal activities were shocked and catapulted off course by the disorder and chaos imposed by the ramifications of a pandemic and the uncertainties it projected.

Seemingly overnight, what was known became the unknown.

Companies that continuously create methods for ethical contingency in response to crises moved to demonstrate responsibility and resiliency. Crisis responses are often manifest via acts of compassion. For example, the DNA testing firm 23andMe went into immediate "care overdrive" when the pandemic hit. A special team was formed to attend to the specific needs of their employees, with solutions designed to help them and their families (offering extended leave, supplemental pay, communication support, etc.). Other companies, regardless of their stated commitment to employees and other stakeholders, ignored obvious ways to support them. Role models are organizations that continue to protect the health, safety, and welfare of their stakeholders and compassionately manage decisions on a daily basis, regardless of the circumstances. This is no small task, as operations have to deal with terminations and shutdowns (education, hotels, airlines, cruise lines, bars, restaurants, etc.).

As in prior periods of wartime crisis, ethical leadership is needed. Given the oppressive circumstances, there is a renewed focus on inclusion, transparency, and care. As threats to our lives and livelihoods have abruptly emerged in ways that we could have never imagined, issues of health and well-being are now more acutely salient. What's more, the disparity of equality is being recognized like never before.[10] With your help, positive organizational ethical development and transformational change can emerge at the intersection of business and society. By exercising ethics, companies can rebuild themselves and start again, drawing upon an increased focus on moral strength. We can choose to deliberately embrace inclusion, cooperation, empathy, moral courage, and other human virtues that sustain and fortify humanity, helping one another to rebound from adversity.

If we hope to turn things around, establishing ethical authenticity in business, we cannot solely rely upon the government and nonprofits to carry the burden. When organizations and their investors expect to benefit from capitalism, they must recognize that

they bear a responsibility to generate positive impacts for their employees, the communities they serve, and the natural environment they inhabit.

Given the economic uncertainties in today's market-place, those who exercise moral strength will be more likely to stay the course by garnering stakeholder respect and commitment. Rather than strategically reaching for a short-term grab, ethical leadership means creating a playbook for business that adopts long-term socially responsible tactics. Emerging from the pandemic, people learned things about them-selves, and those they worked with and for.

Will we apply and retain this learning, or go back to business as usual?

As with the ebb and flow of any era, companies are des-tined to come and go. We will see some organizations dissolve, while others will recast their strategies and come back stronger than before. Innovators will spark new ideas, springing forth novel forms of value. Regard-less of the circumstances, remember one thing. Your purpose and work ethic can never be taken away from you. Your best self is with you at the start of each day.

Business ethics starts at your door.

Strength #1: "Business" and "ethics" are words that belong together. For a successful union, they must genuinely serve one another.

Notes

1 Room, T. (November 18, 2020). Apple to pay $113 million to settle state investigation into iPhone 'batterygate'. Downloaded from: https://www.washingtonpost.com/technology/2020/11/18/apple-fine-battery/.

2 Milenkovic, J. (February 11, 2020). How many iPhones have been sold worldwide? – iPhone sales analyzed. Download from: https://kommandotech.com/statistics/how-many-iphones-have-been-sold-worldwide/.

3 Apple Inc. (September, 2017). *iPhone X environmental report*. Downloaded from: https://www.apple.com/environment/pdf/products/iphone/iPhone_X_PER_sept2017.pdf.

4 Ethical Consumer. (April 23, 2020). Is Apple ethical? *Ethical Consumer*. Downloaded from: https://www.ethicalconsumer.org/company-profile/apple-inc.

5 Schechner, S. (April 30, 2021). EU charges Apple with app store antitrust violations in Spotify case. *The Wall Street Journal*. Downloaded from: https://www.wsj.com/articles/apple-faces-eu-antitrust-charges-over-app-store-payments-in-spotify-case-11619777595.

6 McKay, T. (January 2, 2020). Former Google exec says he was forced out for opposing company's pivot to evil. *Gizmodo*. Downloaded from: https://gizmodo.com/former-google-exec-says-he-was-forced-out-for-opposing-1840777699.

7 Archer, j. (May 21, 2018). Google removes 'don't be evil' from its code of conduct. *The Telegraph*. Downloaded from: https://www.telegraph.co.uk/technology/2018/05/21/google-removes-dont-evil-code-conduct/.

8 Kan, M. (January 3, 2020). Former Google exec: 'Don't be evil' motto is dead. *Entrepreneur*. Downloaded from: https://www.entrepreneur.com/article/344493.

9 Certified B Corporation. (April 23, 2020). About B Corps. *Certified B Corporation: Serving a global community of people using businesses as a force for good*. Downloaded from: https://bcorporation.net/about-b-corps.

10 Ethical Systems. (April 23, 2020). *What is an ethical system? Ethical Systems.org*. Downloaded from: https://www.ethicalsystems.org/.

2   It's all about you

Survival.

Staying alive is central in what makes us human. Sure, we're motivated to help others along the way. But we're often driven to do so because it helps us achieve our own goals. We cooperate to get along in harmony with others, so that our chances of survival (or success) can increase.

It is natural to want to protect our family, tribe, or group.

This mammalian proclivity also helps us at work. Our ability to cooperate effectively with our fellows is important when we're on a team, working in a group, or competing in an entrepreneurial venture.

We're in business to succeed.

So "game on"—let's get out there and score!

By the same token, these innate drives also fuel judgments that can lead to unethical behaviors. Thoughts,

DOI: 10.4324/9780429324284-3

feelings, and actions that prompt exclusion, stereo-typing, discrimination, racism, and a host of unethi-cal and even illegal activities may prevent our best moral selves from taking the lead.

This is why education and practice in personal awareness, reflection, and judgment is so critical—that is, if we want to value ethical action in the work-place and in business enterprise. Just as we have the motivation to look out for ourselves, we also have a powerful drive to care for one another. We are social creatures that have evolved to cooperate and there-fore are interdependent.

During the "shelter-in-place" period brought on by the global pandemic, many of us realized, perhaps for the first time, just how much we enjoy being out and about and in the company of our fellow human beings. As we reorganize our workplace environments, we need to intentionally seek out ways to foster our need to be communal. However we come together, it's important that we create contexts that bring out the best in us, in particular, our moral selves.

You have choices, the ability to direct your own path.

Do you have the desire to take charge of your choices?

That's a critical question that only you can answer.

You have untapped power, personal strengths that can support your ability to change, learn, develop, and grow at any moment. The human brain is an amazing learning organism capable of expansion and rejuvenation. But we forget how easily automaticity and laziness can kick in. We can allow the world around us to dictate what's important to us.

Fred, Mick, Stormy, Bum, Mrs. Cat, and King George

Take a moment to think about what you truly care about.

Just now, I happened to recall some furry friends that made their way into my life. Pets (my own and other people's) have brought me great joy.

Your turn. Kick back and think about what you care about deep down. Consider some cherished moments.

What do you value in life?

Answer honestly, rather than writing down what you think you should say. Just off the top of your head, note three things that are deeply important to you:

1. _____

2. _____

3. _____

_____

Why did you choose these three things?

What is it you value about them in particular?

Why are they important to your well-being?

Most humans have experienced a moment, hopefully many, when we feel that our lives have genuine meaning and purpose. Having just listed some key aspects in your life that you deeply value, you have hopefully experienced a bit of gratitude. Gratitude is a feeling that stems from a sense of appreciation. In recognition of something you care about and value, you are likely to experience a sense of warmth, groundedness, a spaciousness in the chest or heart, and a smile or tears may emerge. It's a kind of rush of goodness from within. If we're lucky, we have friends and family we care about, people that we love and who love us. Despite the burnt dinners, political disagreements, monetary losses, health challenges, dirty diapers, procrastinated projects, and so forth...we carry on.

It's worth it!

Because no one has a crystal ball to determine "what will happen," we tend to draw from a faith or lean on some source of understanding or meaning. We lean into a religion, spirituality, nature, or self-reliance to give us strength to deal with the unknown. During the Covid-19 pandemic of 2020, everyone around the world was shockingly reminded of the delicate nature of our own vulnerability and mortality.

To get through life, we need resources that help us make sense of things that are unexplained, unexpected, and unfair. We need a process that helps provide us with reasoning when we just don't have enough information to really know how or why things happen.

The idea of having a faith in something outside the self to guide morality is not a belief to which everyone ascribes. There are those like Nietzsche, who, as a nihilist, doubted the legitimacy of this idea. He believed there was no substance to traditional social, political, religious, and moral values. Denying that such values had any objective validity, or imposed any binding obligations, he posed this question:

> *Is man merely a mistake of God's? Or God merely a mistake of man?*[1]

Nietzsche basically tossed out the idea of good versus evil as the basis for driving our moral standards. He suggested that we should make decisions and shape our behavioral responses by working to achieve life and species preservation.[2]

Wow! That sounds pretty good to me!

Alas, there's an inherent problem with this approach. Nihilism is often associated with pessimism, which, ironically, when taken to the extreme, condemns existence. A true nihilist would believe in nothing, have no loyalties or purpose, and therefore be very likely to give up or have an impulse to destroy.

OK, so now that doesn't sound very appealing at all.

If Nietzsche and the Joker from Batman (another famous nihilist) are right, that really nothing matters and everything is meaningless, you can stop reading right now.

I'm waiting a few seconds for you to decide.

Hopefully, someone besides my mother and the editor will keep reading.

Are you still there?

OK. Good!

Let's broaden this up and consider another philosophy. A virtue ethicist, like Aristotle, might suggest

"The whole is greater than the sum of its parts"

we think about life by considering our own human (or personal) strengths, as well as the strengths that emerge from human interdependence.

He explained how, "Knowing yourself is the beginning of all wisdom," adding, "The whole is greater than the sum of its parts."

Even if there is some truth to what Nietzsche and the Joker say, it's important to try and overcome this ideology and commit to believing in the value of living the good life by actively pursuing it. Do you want to flourish or simply exist?

If you're in the business world, it's important to find meaning and purpose in what you're doing.

That is, unless you want to live a life of unhappiness.

Of course <u>you want to be happy</u>!

Together, as members of the business community, we can leverage our work efforts to create meaningful relationships. This will fortify our ability to establish purpose and value. This, by the way, is right in line with Aristotle's philosophical ideology.

The act is the reward

Despite the fact that unethical and/or bad things happen in the world, we carry on.

Sometimes work is work.

We all have to engage in tasks that may be difficult, chores that require labor. Sometimes we have to do the heavy lifting (figuratively, but maybe literally speaking as well, depending on your job).

The pursuit of joy includes pursuing the difficult, even enduring hard times.

How you perform your job is an extension of your moral identity. It is the representation of your character going out into the world. The act of demonstrating your best self is virtuous. As the Stoics explained, virtue is its own reward. The bottom line: generous people live happier lives.[3]

We may never know if our intentions are wholly good, right, moral, or pure. Nor may we know the outcomes of our actions. But it is essential for health and human happiness to try and do our best. Thomas Merton, an American Trappist monk, described his belief about this idea. While we will never really know if we're doing right, trying to do so matters. He argued that we should concentrate on the value, rightness, and truth in the work we do, rather than on the results.

Congruently, this notion of acting in the direction of right (what is good, true, and moral) is in one's best interest. Acts of goodness will contribute to your own happiness, via establishing meaning and purpose in your life.

> *Isn't that a rather selfish motive for doing the right thing?*

> *Most certainly!*

> *But that's OK!*

Let's face it, as human beings we're largely ego-driven creatures. Sure, there are good people and extraordinary times in our lives, where selflessness kicks in. But for the vast majority of us, it takes effort to act selflessly, and to stand up for what's right (that's why they call it courage). It may not be easy or simple to do the right thing just because we know it's the right thing to do.

> *Virtue is doing something for the sake of doing it "rightly."*

> *You won't be rewarded. You do it for the sake of being virtuous.*

> *The act itself is the reward.*

> *That's precisely Aristotle's messaging.*

I know. Somehow, that seems rather lean. It doesn't feel quite enough. Don't we all want a pat on the back or acknowledgment when we do something really wonderful? I mean, even if it's for virtue's sake alone, it would still be kind of nice to have a wink or a nod that we cracked it.

But there it is.

That's virtuous action.

Here's the magnificent "aha" that you will fully understand through your own actions. If you make virtuous behavior a practice, you'll find that, as a way of life, it is truly rewarding from the inside out.

Ethics is not an afterthought

I spent a year in graduate school trying to find out more about the basis of altruism. At the end of the day (this saves you months in the library), many scholars suggest that humans can never be purely altruistic.[4] While I was initially disappointed by the finding, there's a silver lining.

We're wired to help one another!

If you have a thought of doing a good deed, the notion of not doing that act can trigger feelings of guilt. In which case, you might execute the good deed to avoid feeling guilty for not executing that action. Plus, in all likelihood you're aware of the fact that you'll feel a sense of pride having accomplished a good deed. These hints of feelings, before they even happen, are usually unconscious. They're referred to as prefactual emotions.

The upshot of these cues?

Our emotions will give us insights to steer clear of trouble (fight or flight). But they will also help inform us about how to be a good person, if we start paying attention to them. Moral emotions are connected to our values. Our values tend to subconsciously compete for supremacy, vying for priority. Many times multiple values are desired, but just one takes the helm (for example, making a quick monetary return versus taking time to consider the unintended consequences of our potential actions).

Picture your values in a pyramid.

You only have so many hours in a day. You may value spending time with family, enjoying pleasures like reading, exercising, or going to a sporting event or a concert with friends. But you also need a roof over your head, electricity, and food on the table. So, you work to be sure you have a home. That's a value choice that most of us make every day.

As mammals, we are wired for cooperation. We instinctively want to ensure that our "group" survives and thrives. We value those we love and appreciate, especially our family and friends. But we are simultaneously being influenced by our surroundings. The context, like the workplace, will influence what we value and also shape our behavior. If the focus of the corporation is driving self-interest day in and day out, it should come as no surprise that individuals become less other-focused, more self-centered, and greedier. As a result, exercising the value of your character becomes especially important.[5] You can choose to do the right thing, because you know it will not only help others; it will help you as well.

By exercising your best self, you can:

Feel pride.

Avoid guilt and shame.

Fortify your character through practice.

Be the change you want to see in the world.

To think and act in this way requires practice. Think of it as exercising your morality. To habituate living the values you purport to care about, naturally emerging moral emotions can help support you in this endeavor. We all want to avoid guilt, but we also want to experience the pride that comes with ethical behavior (doing the right thing). In business, you will perpetually make choices that reveal your morality:

What do I care about?

What harm might my acting (or not acting) cause?

What should I do?

How will this decision impact others?

What are the implications of this action over time?

When you act ethically it ultimately benefits you, along with those you work with and for. Being unethical may get you some immediate gains but will also cause harm. Unethical acts rarely play out well in the long run, in terms of health, welfare, happiness, and long-term success.[6]

There's good news!

Research shows that ethical people are more satisfied in life.[7]

For the skeptics out there, it's fair to second-guess this statement. It does not mean all things go well for you. Rather, it means you aspire to achieve virtuous goals such as gratitude, fortitude, and/or moral courage. Nor does it assume that it's a fair playing field. It suggests and implies that whoever you are, choosing a path of goodness will, in the end, bring greater satisfaction.[8] Given that's the case, we need to better understand what contributes to (or deters us from) ethical behavior at work, affirming why "doing the right thing" is in everyone's best interest.

Being ethical pays off.

It shows up in your reputational and relational capital. It's manifest in your feelings of self-worth. However, many people, especially those of us who are in business, tend to be impatient.[9] We want profits and rewards today, not tomorrow, next month, or sometime in the future. Learning to view ethics as a long-term investment in establishing returns over time is central toward achieving business ethics. Recognizing this factor is critical; that is, if we expect the firm to be moral as it strives to achieve its strategic goals.

Plus, you can sleep at night!

Morality is an organic element of our existence. It is not static, as some compliance approaches might signal. For ethics to be appreciated it has to be valued. Moreover, it's a skill that needs to be exercised regularly to be reliably available when needed.

Reliability means consistency.

People can depend upon you to demonstrate ethical behavior because you don't waver. Making ethical decisions isn't about deciding to be ethical or not. It's about determining how you will deploy the most effective response to the task or problem at hand. While I have had students who have disagreed with me, the definition of an ethical person is not someone who simply chooses *not* to engage in an illegal activity.

Sigh.

Moral action requires a commitment to pay attention to the ethical features of each decision. It's not a matter of convenience or simply reacting to a problem once corporate malfeasance demands attention. To be ethical at work, all your decisions need to be mindful of the preestablished goal to exercise your personal and organizational values. That means considering others, not just yourself. There needs to be an ongoing affirmation of your willingness and interest to be ethical. This desire is shaped by sincere and deliberate intent, as a part of who you are and want to continue to be. This means allocating additional time in deliberation when making decisions. This is time well

spent, as it is an investment in the present, as well as the future.

Ethics is not an afterthought, something you consider when you're in trouble and striving to justify an inappropriate choice that you, or those you work with, have already enacted.

It's a personal decision to want to be ethical.

Then it's living out that choice through regular deliberate practice.

Philosophers have spent centuries crafting theories to depict what they believed to be the "right" path to moral action. In truth, there is rarely one right path to ethical behavior. It is important to have multiple ways of knowing about and being in the world. Moreover, you need to have the skill sets that support the ability to exercise your moral identity. Respecting others is about being aware of and embracing alternative perspectives. What is right can vary, given the person, situation, and context. It's important to appreciate other perspectives, while honoring rules that have been codified.

Although laws are imposed to govern and guide our behavior, business further shapes societal norms.

'But officer, we were going to implement our new ethics code next week.'

Thus, we can see how a cultural psyche of short-term thinking, greed, selfishness, and a general malaise toward the value of moral restraint emerged in our world. Sadly, this can undermine the human value of self-regulation and the worth we assign it in our own lives.

> *Given that self-regulation is our core moral muscle, it's time for a workout!*

The classic piece by Alexander Pope, entitled *Essay on Man*, encourages each of us to "Act well your part, there all the honour lies."[10] This passage suggests that defining and upholding your character is a personal duty. This is the essence of the term honor.

You're it.

The presence of ethics in today's culture is up to you. If you care about acting in the best interest of yourself and other's well-being, you'll see how "doing the right thing" can have a favorable lasting impact. This is not just in the workplace, but much more broadly.

Being ethical helps you create a world that's worth living in.

Strength #2: Being ethical is an investment in your own well-being, as you build a healthier workplace and society.

Notes

1 Nietzsche, F. (April 23, 2020). *Goodreads.* Downloaded from: https://www.goodreads.com/quotes/63480-is-man-merely-a-mistake-of-god-s-or-god-merely.
2 Leiter, B. (2020). Nietzsche's moral and political philosophy. *Stanford Encyclopedia of Philosophy* (Spring 2020 ed.), Edward N. Zalta (ed.). Downloaded from: https://plato.stanford.edu/entries/nietzsche-moral-political/.
3 Park, S. Q., Kahnt, T., Dogan, A., Strang, S., Fehr, E., & Tobler, P. N. (2017). A neural link between generosity and happiness. *Nature Communications, 8,* 15964. doi:10.1038/ncomms15964.

4 Cherry, K. (February 8, 2020). How psychologists explain altruistic helpful behaviors. *verywellmind*. Downloaded from: https://www.verywellmind.com/what-is-altruism-2794828.

5 Warsh, D. (May/June, 1989). How selfish are people—really? *Harvard Business Review*. For the Manager's Bookshelf, featuring: *The evolution of cooperation*, Robert Axelrod (1989), New York: Basic Books. Downloaded from: https://hbr.org/1989/05/how-selfish-are-people-really.

6 Wang, L., & Murnighan, J. K. (December 9, 2013). Rich and unhappy—and fine with unethical behavior? *KelloggInsight*. Downloaded from: https://insight.kellogg.northwestern.edu/article/rich_and_unhappy_and_fine_with_unethical_behavior.

7 Jacobs, T. (June 14, 2017). Study: Ethical people more satisfied with life. *Pacific Standard*. Downloaded from: https://psmag.com/social-justice/study-ethical-people-more-satisfied-with-life-36792.

8 Haybron, D. (2007). Life satisfaction, ethical reflection, and the science of happiness. *Journal of Happiness Studies*, *8*(1), 99–138.

9 Paine, L. S. (2000). Does ethics pay? *Business Ethics Quarterly*, *10*(1), 319–330.

10 Pope, A. (1891). *Essay on man. Moral essays and satires*. Edition by Les Bowler. London: Cassell & Co. Downloaded from: https://www.gutenberg.org/files/2428/2428-h/2428-h.htm.

3 Use your power

Your ethical power is the strength of your morality.

That means living the values you say you hold.

Your authentic beliefs, values, and principles are reflected in how you conduct business and who you chose to do business with. To understand this point, consider where you buy products (food, gas, apparel, sundries, etc.) and services (restaurants, streaming, transportation, events, etc.).

What do you enjoy and remember about the firms you do business with? Is there something you particularly value about the companies you frequent? Is there a firm you like to do business with? Why do you prefer them?

Think of where you like to shop, dine, or visit (online or in person) in terms of where you spend your

DOI: 10.4324/9780429324284-4

money. Identify specifically what it is that keeps you coming back, wanting to do business with them again:

1. _____

2. _____

3. _____

   _____

Maybe it's because of the company's location, i.e., they're just convenient. Perhaps it's the only place you can get exactly what you want or need. Maybe it's because of the people you do business with, i.e., the shopping encounter is pleasant.

To me, when a company stands behind their products and services, I believe they're more trustworthy. This kind of commitment to whatever they're selling means they're reliable. You can count on the item or service being what it purports to be.

This kind of authenticity is something that people appreciate. When you are satisfied, you tell others about your purchase, and you don't hesitate to buy from that company again.

Learning from experience

Personal experiences are how we learn. This is referred to, quite literally, as "experiential learning." To illustrate the process, I'll continue to share some of my personal "moments of learning." You will see how introspection and self-assessment can be used to shape and refine your own standards and principles over time.

In general, people tend to remember the peaks and valleys—that is, the best and the worse of our encounters. So, let's begin with something positive! In this case, the name Vitamix comes to mind. It's a privately held high-end performance blender manufacturer. They stand behind the quality of their product.

I bought a blender from them, and it works great. I swear, it's like a jet engine is taking off as it grinds up frozen fruits and vegetables. But when I happened to encounter a problem with the gadget, they were pleased to address it. I called and explained the handle was splitting, and they said, "Sure, we'll replace the part." That was easily a year after I bought it. Not only do I like the machine, but I feel that the company believes in their product, enough to stand behind its quality and durability. What's more, they genuinely support their customers' needs.

Now that's a memorable consumer experience.

It was so unique, I've told my friends about it.

I even mentioned it in this book!

In today's world of poor quality, throwaway goods, and "it is what it is" everything, this consumer experience is all too rare. For example, I recently took a product back, shortly after I bought it. Before it even made it out of the box, I received an email invitation to buy a warranty. It was an insurance policy to cover parts and service in case the product broke in the first two years of its use.

What came to mind...

If this thing breaks through normal use within a reasonable period of time, why should I have to pay to have it fixed? The product should work, right? If it doesn't, why am I buying insurance on a piece of junk that doesn't serve its purpose? Insurance in this case is a "bet" that the product will break.

I was so irritated, I took it back and said, "No thanks, I'll live without it." As far as I'm concerned, if a company cannot stand behind their product for five minutes without more money, they can keep it.

These examples are sadly in abundance.

My husband went to Home Depot to buy a drill. Preparing for the tool's first job, he removed the tape from the box and was excited to deploy the tool in its maiden voyage.

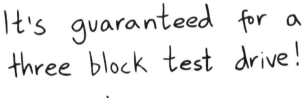

Instead of having a drill to help him with the screws, he was the one getting screwed.

There was no drill in the box!

Oh, there were screws and a recharging station. But no drill! When he took it back, the store manager acknowledged they had sold him a display box.

This shouldn't happen.

Where was the quality control?

What's more, the firm obviously didn't value his (the customer's) time. It was a stressful unnecessary problem that did not have to occur.

Product representation and quality matters to me.

Does this matter to you?

How a company treats its customers is a part of the transaction.

Does this matter to you?

When the company you work for, or are doing business with, provides respect, offers open communication, and takes the time to ensure a positive customer experience, you appreciate it. We want to work for companies that treat people right. As consumers, we want to do business with these kinds of companies today, and in the future.

The flip side

There are definite standouts in terms of positive encounters. Trader Joe's is a grocery chain that comes to mind. With 300 stores nationwide and more than $3 billion in annual revenue, it's surprising how they maintain such friendly and personalized service.

The key is in their employees. They're essentially ambassadors for support, demonstrating consistency in customer care. They are *relentless* (purposeful word choice here) in making sure you are always satisfied. Having shopped there for many years, on the rare occasion that an issue occurs, their solution is always swift and accompanied by goodwill. I've received assistance to my car, taxi/ride, or bike, when needed. During the pandemic, they immediately imposed special safety measures. This included staying positive as everyone stepped up to honor social distancing and other precautions to protect shoppers and organizational members. Especially noteworthy is this company's uniformity in terms of its dependability. You can stop at a Trader's in downtown Washington, DC, Pacific Grove, CA, Manhattan, NY, or Westlake, OH, and you know they will have the same kinds of quality products and services.

Sometimes a favorable business deal might come from where you least expect it, like buying a used car. Armed with my Carfax data and having done my homework on the make/model of interest, I contacted the head of the sales department at our local Mazda dealership. Now, when I say I did my homework, I mean conducting some research. I knew the precise statistics on what this car was selling for throughout the nation (along with trends over the past few years), along with the nuances of its reliability and safety via various government and consumer reporting services.

When the manager was on the phone, I stated plainly that I was going to make a purchase decision within a week. If he remained ethical and forthright, we could close in short order. But if, at any time, I felt that business ethics was not front and center, or that he was not being straight with me, the transaction would be immediately over. No turning back.

As you might expect, there were a series of negotiations. After a few minor physical details were corrected on the vehicle, we moved to discuss the financial terms. We both modified our positions several times on price, then closed. The neat thing about buying a car today is that if you do your homework, you can get a pretty good idea of what the profit margins are. Then you are able to decide what you think is a fair deal. In the end, he made money and I was satisfied.

I enjoy writing about positive experiences. I appreciate the benefits of smooth sailing. The absence of problems has come to be noteworthy these days. Just a simple transaction that goes as planned, no issues or errors, is a welcomed encounter. Instead of being anomalies or "one-off" encounters, negative incidents are starting to become the norm. Consider your cable, phone, Internet, banking, utility, healthcare, or insurance providers. Reflect for a moment on some of the experiences you have with other service providers (e.g., ride sharing, airlines). How about doing business with your basic retailers (e.g., CVS, Macy's, Amazon), or other platforms that have become woven into the fabric of your everyday life?

Are you generally pleased with their products and services?

Are you typically delighted with your customer experience?

If your response to the above is "yes," I would argue that you may have been lulled into a false sense of acceptance and consumer malaise. Or maybe you have figured out a way to buy perfect products. If that's the case, please let me know! My email address: *lsekerka@menlo.edu.*

Perhaps your consumption is limited. This may be because of your means. But it could be because of a personal decision to be socially responsible (i.e., buying more stuff isn't necessary).

Hats off to you if that's the case.

For those who are consuming responsibly, there is recognition that buying less is better for the natural environment. Many of us can improve by becoming more attentive to ethical consumption and demand this approach from those we choose to do business with.

Of course, this takes time.

By shaping the demand, companies are starting to realize they cannot get away with gaming consumers. For example, I recently took financial institutions to task, calling both USAA and Bank of America.

The former company sent an erroneous letter demanding additional collateral for a loan I had already secured for that used car I was telling you about earlier. They apologized for the error and corrected what turned out to be a data analytics issue. The latter company charged international fees for purchases made on the Internet that were not transparent prior to exacting them. They were removed.

You might ask, "Who has time for this?" I would say that if you do not make time for it, you'll continue to get ripped off, and so will everyone else. Sadly, for many people, their expectations have become so low they no longer care (or never knew you could care) about product and consumer quality, truth in advertising, and/or consumer respect.

I would also add that if you're not thinking about this concern as a personal ethical problem, you have not really considered the implications of monopolies and oligarchies.

While Americans currently benefit from features central to democratic governance (e.g., elections, freedom of speech, freedom to associate), our policies are often dominated by powerful businesses and a small number of affluent Americans.[1] This is a part of what we're seeing with rampant bimodal wealth distribution in the West. This issue has palpable implications for things you care about, like wages, income, health, quality of life, and so forth.

The consequences for business and society are inseparable, and the forces of the few in power are becoming even more powerful. Between 1976 and 2012, the share of U.S. income earned by the top 1% almost tripled, rising from 9% to 24%.[2]

TRICKLE DOWN ECONOMICS EXPLAINED

@ CARTOONRALPH

There is a connection between the influence on public policy of big corporations and the wealthy who control them, and the way business treats their customers. Unless firms make a commitment to genuinely care about their consumer relationships, they will invariably short-change their patrons. Companies gradually or blatantly cut out the assumption of respect, which is the ethics of customer relations. Or, as we say in business ethics, *stakeholder management*.

Here are some explicit illustrations of this point:

- Has your phone or cable arrangement ever been changed without your being notified (aside from your bill mysteriously skyrocketing)?

- Have you ever bought a ticket on a plane that was oversold? Or did the airline change your flight to suit their convenience?
- Have you accidentally bought outdated or tasteless food?
- Did your prepaid ride stiff you?
- Have you bought something "on sale," only to get home and see that you were charged full price?
- Has a box from Amazon arrived empty?

I recently learned that the Romaine lettuce I just ate had been recalled for salmonella. A week later, the indigestion pills my husband takes were recalled for including potentially dangerous levels of a carcinogenic compound. And then, I received an email from a law firm indicating they would represent me for the cancer that these Zantac pills might cause.

These are not accidents or serendipitous occurrences. These recalls, like so many unethical issues, are the result of sloppy, shoddy, hurried, and careless practices. We are, quite literally, swallowing the lack of ethics in business. And it can kill us!

We are all experiencing these issues in our own lives.[3]

Some of us perceive or notice them more than others. While seemingly minuscule in the moment, even the most modest of concerns, when multiplied by the thousands, add up to an inordinate amount of unethical slack. This void is something that companies count on your not paying attention to. If you did, it would cost them money.

Dealing with these issues can be time-consuming and irritating. When mishaps occur, it may seem like it's not worth the hassle to address. That's ultimately money out of your pocket and into theirs. Money that you didn't agree to give corporations that they will happily take from you, me, and everyone else.

When have you encountered this sort of experience?

Think of a few examples and describe what happened and why you think it was an ethical issue:

1. _____

2. _____

3. _____

   _____

A few stolen pennies won't matter

These little drips of money remind me of the classic *Office Space* movie, where the plot line involves Peter, Michael, and Samir who create a penny-shaving scheme to retaliate against their organization. Given that the firm they work for decides to lay off hard-working employees, the friends find a way to get back at the software company by stealing from it in miniscule increments. It might have gone unnoticed, but a bug in the software accidentally increases the amount they intended to steal, exponentially (note the irony that the software company's software had bugs).

When we ignore the little drips, they turn into an absence of ethical authenticity.

How does your organization treat its customers?

Does your organization care about its employees?

Another way to determine if a company is ethical is to see how it treats its employees. Sure, you can look at Glassdoor.com for reviews. That said, I always question the sample: Is it disproportionately composed of negative self-reports?

Reading about the company, its mission, vision, and values, is important. But the authentic moral identity of the company is not just the presence of words like "stakeholders" in its messaging, but in the relational support it demonstrates and how it measures performance.

In a paradoxical shift, the American culture has actually given corporations license to expect an always-"on" workday. In writing for *The Atlantic*, Derek Thompson explains how norms in the West have changed over the decades to create a society where work has become the source of our identity. He explains how, over time, the college elite have recast the notion of work from a place where you go to accomplish a set of goals, to a platform where you create a sense of self. This is how the job, for some, has become a sort of religion, i.e., promising fulfillment, transcendence, and community.[4]

Welcome the emergence of "workism."

Additional pressure to manage one's identity as a sort of personal brand, requiring cultivation and maintenance, has simply promulgated the reality of work becoming a 24/7 job.

Part of management's job is to inculcate human sentiments into the practices, processes, and culture of the firm. Organizations reflect the values and beliefs of those who lead them. The corporation, in and of itself, has no soul.[5] It's just a legal document. As such, it cannot offer care, empathy, or respect.

It is simply an organized structure, put together to achieve a goal.

Management is not just a science.

When executed it is about living one's character, being a good person, and helping others to do the same.[6]

If employees are cast merely as the means to an end (increasing shareholder value, creating wealth for executives, increasing market share), workism thrives.

Worse yet, work is seen as the goal itself.

This is a trick. People are not cogs!

People are the embodiment of virtues, values, and sentiments that support an organization's ability to thrive.

Many companies do not reinforce the value of having a personal life. Over time, many Americans have forgotten (or it never occurred to them) that a key purpose of work is to buy free time!

Scholars who specialize in the study of happiness have shown many times over that people find the most joy by spending time with their friends, family, and partners.[7] Does your organization enable you to have a life away from the office to focus on relationships, hobbies, and personal life?

By "away" I mean totally unplugged from the Internet. No checking your emails/messages, making phone calls, and attending to catch-up duties. I mean your full and unmitigated attention is on your own life, separate from your work.

> *Does your organization treat people with respect?*

> *Does your organization give lip-service to its values (e.g., authenticity, quality, care, and commitment)?*

When companies are just mechanisms for profit, their stated values of care can go right out the window.

A few stolen millions won't matter

The Wells Fargo Bank (WFB) fraud scandal represents blatant corporate hypocrisy. In 2016, the bank's customers started noticing unanticipated fees and unrequested lines of credit appearing on their statements. When this fraud scandal broke, branch employees were immediately blamed. In actuality, it was the incentive performance programs imposed by top management that prompted the behavioral actions. If workers were to make their quotas, they needed to cross-sell and up their numbers through the creation of bogus accounts.

By the end of 2018, the bank faced civil and criminal lawsuits estimated at $2.7 billion as a result of the fraud. Initially, the bank fired employees who created the accounts. They were the scapegoats for the corporate malfeasance. It took a U.S. Senate investigation led by Senator Elizabeth Warren to bring attention to the case, resulting in the resignation of WFB's CEO, John Stumpf.[8]

Hang on, it gets worse.

The bank's management strategized to reap monetary benefits from the scandal, pointing to the fact that "unnamed insurance companies" knew about or consciously disregarded the misconduct.

What?!!!!!

Are you kidding me?

Through shareholder lawsuits, money was recovered for the company. This action determined that insurance

companies had to pay $240 million in liability coverage to the current and former officers and directors, who were named as defendants.[9] So, the bank figured out how to make money off of being in trouble, after making unethical moves to get their employees to set up fraudulent accounts on behalf of their customers.

OK, wait.

The bank escapes accountability for its violations, then it gets money through the legal system for doing so.

Is that right?

Is that acceptable?

Those involved in the legal case asserted that they "Acted in good faith and in a manner they reasonably believed to be in the best interests of Wells Fargo and its shareholders."[10] While WFB agreed to pay $190 million in fines and restitution, $480 million to settle a shareholder class-action lawsuit, and $142 million to settle a consumer class-action suit, that's chump change for them.

I'm not buying it.

Are you?

When I asked my students how many of them did business with this bank before and after the scandal, only one person left WFB as a result of the company's unethical activity.

This was a disturbing outcome.

It seems that consumers tend to accept a lack of ethics in business. In general, people expect companies to misbehave.

This is a problem.

What many fail to recognize is that consumers are in a relationship with those they choose to do business with. Who you give your money to says something about you. They are, in essence, an extension of your moral identity. So, if you are willing to continue to do business with unethical firms, you are in some ways endorsing and affirming the continuation of their deception. You are ignoring the fact that you, as a consumer, bear some responsibility for ensuring that the firms you do business with maintain respect for ethics in society.

> *If you don't use your moral strength, your power, you give it away.*

> *Consumer malaise is unacceptable.*

> *It actually contributes to a corporation's ability to continue to behave in whatever manner they wish, to make a profit at your expense.*

Returning to the saga at WFB, in February of 2020 the bank agreed to pay a $3 billion settlement for charges brought by the U.S. Justice Department and the Securities and Exchange Commission. The bank's aggressive sales goals led to widespread consumer abuse, including millions of accounts being opened without consent. The bank acknowledged that it had collected millions of dollars in fees, motivating its employees to falsify records, forge signatures, and misuse customer personal information to open fake accounts to meet unrealistic sales goals. According to the settlement, bank leaders knew of the behavior, but did nothing to stop it until 2016. The fine was about 15% of the bank's $19.5 billion profit in 2019.

Missing from this corporate penalty is the fact that it did not cover individual employees (the white-collar leaders who created the platform for unethical performance). As with the mill of corporate fraud scandals, the people who instigated the plan, the senior bank officials involved, were never criminally charged.[11] Some might say this is justice. The punitive actions were modest, to say the least. The bank's stock suffered a blow during the scandal, but it essentially bounced right back.

Without the voice of a few customers who eventually complained, the WFB scandal would have continued

to have grown bigger. The problem is that we, the consumers, rarely demand that our business partners hold ethical standards. In this particular case, we let a financial institution be cavalier with our money. One would think that a bank would be a trusted institution, not a firm whose reliability you would have to second-guess.

Instead of shutting them down, their unethical behavior was rewarded in 2008, with the bailout during the financial crisis. So, why would institutional leaders learn to behave any differently? While the motives may have been to head off a collapse of the market, we inadvertently ended up reinforcing their bad behavior. Are we so accepting that firms can do whatever they want, whenever they want, that we don't care? I think we have to start taking action, holding the firms that we do business with accountable for their actions. While money may win you more money, it cannot take your power, unless you give it away. Where you put your money is an expression of your moral identity.

Use your power!

Use your moral strength!

Amazon is another company that gives us an opportunity to consider our role in shaping ethics within business. The online retail conglomerate has a valuation of $1 trillion and is considered the largest global marketplace, having literally redefined how people shop and sell goods.

Their activity now influences employment, investment, government policy, and global economics writ large. While Amazon states stakeholders are important to them, they seem to pick and choose when they opt to "care" for their needs. A few examples, which make the point, include Amazon's:

✓ Focus on expedited shipping with little immediate regard for greenhouse gas emissions and pollutants such as carbon dioxide

✓ Use of cheap capital and gatekeeping power over customers and increasingly using fulfillment procedures that exploit small businesses, merchants, farmers, and authors

✓ Delay in paying competitive wages and benefits to warehouse workers

✓ Organizational culture of competition, which may drive litigation in cases of workplace abuse, discrimination, and maltreatment

✓ Opposition of worker protections and rights via unionization

✓ Tech campuses that often displace working-class Black and Latino communities[12]

Taking these examples together, what does this mean?

What can you do?

Deliberately take steps to live the values you say you hold.

We all need to pitch in. Start making decisions and engaging in actions that represent our best selves and ensure that our character is deliberately exercised. That means being more thoughtful in making decisions about who we do business with, how we do business, and where we work.

Are you employed by a company like Amazon?

Do you do business with firms like WFB?

You may or may not have the option to choose who you work for. But you can think about how you continue to direct your power by putting your time and talent toward organizations that care about their stakeholders.

I mean genuinely care, not just advertise it.

Your power is in applying deliberate thought to where you put your time, talent, and money. You can choose to do business with whomever you wish. If it's an oligarchy like cable, you can opt out, not buy into their "on demand."

> *I mean, how many reruns of "The Big Bang Theory" do you really need to see?*

You CAN unplug from some of these "must-have" services. When I want to see something (e.g., *The Crown, Game of Thrones, Schitt's Creek*), I can procure it. But I have learned to wait a few months, and get it for free! Much of today's programming is available at your local library at no cost (all of the above shows, for example). These are the very same services as what you pay for! I realize you might not be able to text your friends about the episode that night or the next day. But you have options.

I'm just saying...

> *You might have to wait a few weeks. But you cannot miss what you haven't seen yet.*

If it's really all "that," the program will always be available; within a short period of time, it's basically free.

I'm not saying it's unethical to charge for streaming services. What I am saying is are you seriously questioning yourself on where you invest your money? Ask yourself:

- How much of your service is reliable and dependable?
- Are streaming programs today a "need" or a "want?"
- If it's a "want," is this money something that might be better spent on something you "need?"

- Have these companies cornered the market in such a way that you feel you have few options?

This is just one example, and a simple description of how I've responded to dealing with one oligarchical industry. We all have a multitude of choices and options. Just take a stand and start somewhere.

Use the power of your consumer dollar as a vote for business ethics.

Again, do you want to improve the bottom lines of firms that treat you with respect and stand behind their products? Or do you want to increase the wealth of those who make their money on the backs of others, unethically?

As Greta Thunberg's prophetic leadership asks of us, we must "choose to choose" what we care about. The young Swedish environmental activist explained to the world that we must take action in the direction of our values now, today. As *Time Magazine's* 2019 "Person of the Year", she was heralded for drawing global attention to humanity's predatory relationship with the earth.[13]

Big companies will only face consequences for their actions if people work together to make demands of them. Collectively, consumers can stand up to the unethical behavior of "the corporation" and work together to demand positive change.

> *Stakeholders have used their power to change entire industries.*

What would Mr Tuna say?

Think about the dolphin-safe tuna you see on every grocery store shelf today. Prior to 1990, this was not the case. In the U.S., the Earth Island Institute motivated tuna companies to agree to catch fish without setting nets on or near dolphins. The Institute provided the world with the first video footage of dolphins being killed by typical fishing practices used at the time.

Consumers were outraged and rallied to back the move to protect these much-loved mammals. New standards were subsequently incorporated into the Marine Mammal Protection Act, which now protects 99% of the dolphin population from fishing nets today.[14]

This positive change (look for the dolphin-safe picture on the next can of tuna fish you buy) was the direct result of collective activism.

Fast (unethical) fashion

Now, think about the clothes you buy.

We need to demand more from the apparel industry.

Brands that expeditiously produce pieces to crank out new styles and get them to market quickly are referred to as "fast fashion." Companies that produce them optimize aspects of the supply chain to manufacture goods cheap and quick, with a goal to encourage consumption. Buying more goods of less quality more often is not sustainable for people or the planet.

Every year, about 150 tons of clothing and shoes are sold worldwide. The majority of it eventually ends up in landfills or is incinerated. This process wastes valuable resources and causes harm to the natural environment. It's a business model based upon a lack of forethought and prudent consumption. Corporations are often strategic about externalizing their costs, so that other entities (people and the planet) bear the brunt of their wasteful activities.

In short, firms profit at the expense of others.

Externalizing costs means that companies increase their margins by having society and the natural environment pay for them. The current shareholder and finance models often reward firms that behave in this manner.[15] A lack of consumer awareness has contributed to a lack of collection structures and a supply chain based on "take-make-waste" standards in the industry.[16] But with more advocacy, from groups like *Recycle Nation*, some firms have begun to move toward a "cradle-to-grave" business model. The Sustainable Development Goals (SDGs) endorsed by the United Nations (UN) include "Responsible

Consumption and Production" (Goal 12). The UN de-scribes this as follows:

> Promoting resource and energy efficiency, sus-tainable infrastructure, and providing access to basic services, green and decent jobs, and a bet-ter quality of life for all. Its implementation helps to achieve overall development plans, reduce fu-ture economic, environmental, and social costs, strengthen economic competitiveness, and re-duce poverty.[17]

As material consumption of our natural resources increases, we face a systemic global challenge with

regard to how we're going to each assume responsibility for our air, water, and soil pollution.

Aiming to do more and better with less, overall welfare gains through business and economic activities will stem from the reduction of resource use, degradation, and pollution within an entrepreneurial life cycle, while increasing well-being and quality of life. There is a critical need to focus on our supply chain, involving everyone from producer to consumer. This means consumer education regarding sustainable consumption and lifestyles, providing leaders at every age with information, standards, labels, and regulatory efforts to fortify sustainable public procurement, use, and ongoing innovation.

Rather than heading to the landfill, materials like rubber, plastics, and textile fibers can be recovered to minimize the impact of clothing manufacturing and disposal. PUMA has role-modeled this business behavior by creating their "Bring me Back" initiative and "InCycle" product line to address the concern that 57% of its impact on the environment came from raw materials in their shoes and clothing.

They took this statistic as a wakeup call to find new ways to decrease their reliance on the use of virgin

resources and to innovate sustainable manufacturing techniques.[18]

Take the money and run?

Reflect for a moment on where you spend your time, money, and talent. List three things you can do over the course of the next week to make companies listen to your concerns.

Think about it.

If you're having trouble getting started, think about a billing error or when a surprise fee showed up on your account. Recall a time when you bought a product and it fell apart or did not perform according to expectations. Perhaps you ordered an item and it never arrived. Are you concerned about the natural environment and want to see a change in how something is made, packaged, or delivered?

Now list some ways in which you can exercise your power:

1. _____

2. _____

3. _____

_____

Every company has a consumer relations address, email, and telephone number. Set aside time to make some calls to the firms you do business with. Make your values known! Fill out those never-ending surveys they send you with some qualitative comments about the things that YOU care about (e.g., make more durable products that can be repaired/reused).

Remember you can always exercise your values by choosing *not* to buy. Spend some time reading about alternatives and how to become a more informed consumer. Cutting back on your consumables is an effective way to reduce your carbon footprint.

Carpe diem!

Get involved by taking part in consumer activist groups, targeted NGOs, and collectives, working in concert with others who share similar concerns. People just like you have influenced (and continue to make an impact on) entire industries.

Exercise your ethics by making meaningful
and lasting positive change where you work.

If you are an investor, you can flex your moral muscles by choosing to direct your funds to companies that reflect your moral identity.

Such efforts can help drive the value of moral strength within the broader market, which can redefine the nature of capitalism. Many scholars and business leaders believe that a new form of capitalism is needed. Bipartisan legislation is required to address social issues like healthcare, education, and climate change.

Super-achievers need to be rewarded for their merit, hard work, grit, determination, and enterprise. But continually increasing the fortunes of the world's wealthiest on the backs of the lower and middle classes continues to be a problem. To date, 26 people hold the preponderance of wealth of the entire planet! Billionaire fortunes continue to increase, to the tune of $2.5 billion a day, while the 3.8 billion people who make up the poorest half of humanity watch their share decline annually.[19]

By coupling the forces of share- and stakeholder power, corporate social responsibility can shape how

profits are achieved. Considering morality as a driver of sustainable and responsible profitization, investors can prompt firms to reassert ethics into the process of wealth creation.[20]

There are some demonstrative shifts being made in the apparel, food, and recycling sectors globally. Think about the emergence of sustainable clothing, organic food, fair trade coffee, and reusable/renewable energy. Business will change how it sources, makes, and creates its products and services, if consumers (you) invest your time, talent, and money in the value of ethics.

If unethical goods aren't making money,
business will quit making them.

There can be repercussions for companies if they do not address consumer demands for change. In 2020, two out of three consumers choose brands based on how they perceive the company and its products' stand on social issues, up from about half in 2017.[21] Here's the good news: it is easier for consumer stakeholders to get brands to address social problems than to get government action. So use your wallet share to demonstrate your values.

Belief-driven buyers are now the majority across markets, including the U.S. (59%), Japan (60%), the U.K. (57%), and Germany (54%). This orientation is shared across age groups (18–34 (69%), 35–54 (67%), and 55+ (56%)) and income levels (low (62%), middle (62%), and high (69%)).[22] As millennials lead the way, a palpable shift is underway.

Many of my students, colleagues, family, and neighbors have been engaged in efforts to create positive change in a variety of ways. They've responded to online security issues by stepping away from the use of Facebook. They are rethinking the sustainability of their shopping choices, buying less and being more mindful about supply chain ethics. They've taken a stand against fast fashion. They've begun to shift their retirement portfolios toward socially responsible investing. Some are working within their local communities to enhance more effective recycling programs, engaging in environmental conservation and sustainability projects.

At Menlo College in Atherton, CA, undergraduates have eagerly volunteered and engaged in the *Being a Better Bear* reading initiative. This program has helped hundreds of children in the Bay area community become exposed to ethics earlier, in preschool and elementary education.[23]

Learners at every age are beginning to connect the dots. They are seeing how their daily actions, when added up over a lifetime and viewed cumulatively, may not reflect authentic care, compassion, and commitment to the natural environment and all sentient beings. Seeing this disconnect, they want to do something about it.

I have also met people who are still in denial.

Some people are unable to see how they play a role in today's ethical concerns in business. Or perhaps they simply don't care. To them I say, you need to care, because your actions will affect your children, and your children's children. You are a steward of the planet and for the lives of others.

What was freely given to you should be left in the same or better condition.

You can CHOOSE to take the time to make things better, remedy the harms, and begin to address the issues and concerns that are around you. This is your time, and it's your society, culture, and world. You can point out and explain the problems, bring up those ethical issues, and stand up for what you know is right.

*If you're unsure, you can speak up, reach out,
and get help.*

I don't know about you, but I am unwilling to give
away my power. That means, I refuse to give up my
right to make informed choices. I deliberately exercise my moral identity in my daily activities.

I am not willing to let go of my right to decide what's
important, what's of value, and what matters. I give
voice to my values and take action.

Do you?

Strength #3: Expect and demand more from every corporation you do business with.

Notes

1 Gilens, M., & Page, B. I. (September 14, 2014). Testing theories of American politics: Elites, interest groups, and average citizens. *Perspectives on Politics, 12*(3). Downloaded from: https://www.cambridge.org/core/journals/perspectives-on-politics/article/testing-theories-of-american-politics-elites-interest-groups-and-average-citizens/62327F513959D0A304D4893B382B992B.

2 Meyer, C., & Kirby, J. (January 28, 2014). Income equality is a sustainability issue. *Harvard Business Review.* Downloaded from: https://hbr.org/2014/01/income-inequality-is-a-sustainability-issue-2.

3 Sekerka, L. E. (2015). *Ethics is a daily deal: Choosing to build moral strength as a practice.* Springer.

4 Thompson, D. (2019). Workism is making Americans miserable. *The Atlantic, 24.* Downloaded from: https://www.theatlantic.com/ideas/archive/2019/02/religion-workism-making-americans-miserable/583441/?utm_medium=cr&utm_source=email-promo&utm_name=onboarding&utm_term=bau&utm_content=email7.

5 Achbar, M., Simpson, B., Achbar, M., & Abbott, J. (2003). The corporation [Motion picture]. *Canada: Big Picture Media Corporation.*

6 Stewart, M. (2009). *The management myth: Debunking modern business philosophy.* W. W. Norton & Company.

7 Caunt, B. S., Franklin, J., Brodaty, N. E., & Brodaty, H. (2013). Exploring the causes of subjective well-being: A content analysis of peoples' recipes for long-term happiness. *Journal of Happiness Studies, 14*(2), 475–499. Downloaded from: https://link.springer.com/article/10.1007/s10902-012-9339-1.

8 Chappell, B. (September 20, 2016). "You should resign": Watch Sen. Elizabeth Warren grill Wells Fargo CEO John Stumpf. *NPR, The Two-Way.* Downloaded from: https://www.npr.org/sections/thetwo-way/2016/09/20/494738797/you-should-resign-watch-sen-elizabeth-warren-grill-wells-fargo-ceo-john-stumpf.

9 Wack, K. (March 1, 2019). In a twist, Wells Fargo gets $240M payout in a latest phony-accounts settlement. *American Banker.* Downloaded from: https://www.americanbanker.com/news/in-a-twist-wells-fargo-gets-240m-payout-in-latest-phony-account-settlement.

10 Ibid.

11 Merle, R. (February 21, 2020). Wells Fargo reaches $3 billion settlement with DOJ, SEC over face-accounts scandal. *The Washington Post* (Business). Downloaded from: https://www.washingtonpost.com/business/2020/02/21/wells-fargo-fake-accounts-settlement/?utm_campaign=wp_news_alert_revere&utm_medium=email&utm_source=alert&wpisrc=al_news__alert-economy--alert-national&wpmk=1.

12 Stoller, M. (October 4, 2018). Don't thank Bezos for giving Amazon workers a much-needed raise. *The Guardian*. Downloaded from: https://www.theguardian.com/commentisfree/2018/oct/04/jeff-bezos-amazon-workers-raise-monopoly.

13 Felsenthal, E. (December 23, 2019). Time's Editor-in-chief on why Greta Thunberg is the person of the year. Downloaded from: https://time.com/person-of-the-year-2019-greta-thunberg-choice/

14 *IMP*. (April 23, 2020). Dolphin safe fishing. The problem: Protecting dolphins from deadly fishing practices. Save dolphins. Downloaded from: http://savedolphins.eii.org/campaigns/dsf.

15 *Nature and More*. (April 23, 2020). What are "externalized" costs? Downloaded from: https://www.natureandmore.com/en/true-cost-of-food/what-are-externalized-costs.

16 *I:CO*. (April 23, 2020). Positive change requires bold thinking. *I:Colution, rethink, reuse, recycle, renew*. Downloaded from: https://www.ico-spirit.com/en/.

17 *United Nations*. (April 25, 2020). *United Nations sustainable development goals: 12*. Downloaded from: https://www.un.org/sustainabledevelopment/sustainable-consumption-production/.

18 Tardif, R. (March 22, 2013). In-store apparel recycling and a new line of recycled, recyclable clothing and shoes has PUMA thinking green. Cradle-to-Grave sportswear: Puma's bring me back program. *Recycle Nation*. Downloaded from: https://recyclenation.com/2013/03/cradle-grave-sportswear-puma-bring-program/.

19 *Oxfam International*. (January 21, 2019). Billionaire fortunes grew by $2.5 billion a day last year as poorest saw their wealth fall. Downloaded from: https://www.oxfam.org/en/press-releases/billionaire-fortunes-grew-25-billion-day-last-year-poorest-saw-their-wealth-fall.

20 Sekerka, L. E., & Stimel, D. (2019). Business ethics meets economics: Investing in corporations that embrace positive impact. *Global Business & Economics Anthology, 1*, 1–5.

21 Boyle, M. (June 5, 2020). Target's hometown tragedy unearths its struggles with diversity. *BNN Bloomberg*. Downloaded from: https://www.bnnbloomberg.ca/target-s-hometown-tragedy-unearths-its-struggles-with-diversity-1.1446474.

22 Edelman. (October, 2018). Brand take a stand. Edelman research. Downloaded from: https://www.edelman.com/sites/g/files/aatuss191/files/2018-10/2018_Edelman_Earned_Brand_Global_Report.pdf.

23 Sekerka, L. E. (2015). *Being a better bear: What it means to be ethical.* Atherton, CA: Menlo Imprint.

4   Look around

We tend to mirror our surroundings. If honesty, integrity, and courage are valued by the people you work with and for, you're likely to demonstrate those values too.

Who is your employer?

What industry are you in?

What is your workplace environment like?

How do you feel when you go to work?

How are you treated by your co-workers?

Does management drive performance by ethical means?

Does your organization bring out the best in you?

Does the company motivate behaviors that don't rest well with you?

DOI: 10.4324/9780429324284-5

Do you take pride in your work?

Does how "work gets done" at your organization go against the grain of what you know to be right, good, or true?

Are you gratified by what you do?

Does your employer appreciate you?

Let's start with some positives.

Identify three things that you're proud of, something you have accomplished at work. It might be completing a project, hitting a target or goal, or perhaps something related to the people you work with, the team you're on, or the company you work for. Regardless of where you work, you show up, you do your best, and you have achieved things. List a few of your achievements below:

1. _____

2. _____

3. _____

_____

Now, think about the emotions that these recollections engendered. What were you feeling when you experienced these accomplishments?

Typically, pride makes us feel joy, gratification, and a sense of fulfillment. Pride is actually considered a self-conscious emotion because, like shame, guilt, and embarrassment, it supports moral behavior. When these feelings arise, we are prompted to reflect inwardly and evaluate ourselves in reference to personal and external values and standards.[1] As moral emotions, these feelings influence the link between moral standards and moral behavior.

Now, let's go back to the workplace.

If you cannot wait to get the H*** out of there, if you feel like ending your day in the bottom of a whiskey tumbler or engaging in some form of mind-numbing escapism, you might want to consider the ethicality of your job and the environment in which you work.

Human beings naturally adapt to the people they surround themselves with, along with the context and/or situation they are in. Interaction breeds similarity. We know that people are (or become like) those they spend time with.[2,3]

This takes us back to the basic elements of our own survival.

The majority of us will acclimate to the environmental and the social setting we're in. As mammals, we are social creatures. We like to have friends and we all crave a sense of belonging. People in business truly want to be a part of something bigger than themselves. To achieve this, it behooves us to get along.

You know, play well with others.

We have heard that line since kindergarten. But it's still true, especially in the workplace.

In the goldfish bowl together

Prompted by an infusion of technology and generational shifts, we're literally and figuratively an interconnected workplace. In just the last five years, the amount of time employees spend engaging in collaborative work has increased by 50%. That translates into taking over 80% of their time.[4] During that same period, companies like Microsoft found that their employees are now on twice as many teams to accomplish their work goals.[5]

This means we have to rely upon one another to accomplish our jobs. So, if you are who you hang out with, you better be certain that the people you work with and the organization that you work for are bringing out the best in you and that they support your moral identity.

Take a step back and reflect on this for a moment.

Does your company encourage you to be ethical in how you achieve your goals? Or is it all about the race to profits, escalating your primal desire to win, succeed, and make money? Research shows that the people you surround yourself with influence your behavioral habits, value prioritization, and moral or amoral choices.[6]

Take a good look around.

What's it like at your organization?

Do you feel safe, respected, valued, and appreciated?

If you don't feel safe, please get some help immediately!

REALLY.

Reach out to your supervisor or manager, someone in Human Resources, and/or a trusted colleague. Use the resources at your company to report your issue (e.g., anonymous hotline).

You may need to contact an employment lawyer and ask for help.

Everyone deserves respect.

It's not part of a compensation package.

It's a human right.

Organizations that tolerate disrespect enable toxic environments to brew. But it's hard to realize you're a fish when you're in the bowl.

As you look around your organizational bowl, remember, you are (or you become) like those you're swimming with. When ethical issues emerge, including a lack of respect and not being valued or

appreciated, you can choose to numb out and just accept them.

We can all choose to turn a blind eye. We can say, "It's not my job. That's just the way things are."

Not taking action can be easily rationalized.

There are typical thoughts that might go through your head just before you decide to ignore or engage in an unethical act at work:

It won't matter.

Everyone's doing it.

It's not in my job description.

Just this once.

I deserve "_____."

Screw them, they don't pay me enough.

I can't rock the boat and risk losing my job.

No one's looking.

When we think that something is going on that's unethical and we choose to say nothing, we actually become a part of the problem.

In effect, we become enablers of our organization's unethical health if we say or do nothing. Employees who neglect speaking up about ethical issues subtly reaffirm the continuation of the harms occurring. You become an accomplice to the crime.

But I'm keenly aware that there is a massive disjuncture between saying we should all be able to "blow the whistle" and the reality of actually doing so. The rigors of such actions are often oversimplified in their descriptive presentations.

Management has not always consistently valued whistleblowing. The company code may say they want employees to give voice to their values. But when reporters step up, they are not necessarily appreciated. As a result of trailblazers before you, there are now whistleblower laws in place specifically designed to protect the rights of the reporter.

And, sadly, our culture doesn't always view whistleblowing as an act of valor.

Heavy sigh. Now what?

We each have to make a decision about our character.

We have to make that decision BEFORE any ethical issue emerges.

Silent obedience leads to disaster

We have to decide who we want to be in the world and make a commitment to ourselves that this is "who we are" and stick to it. We have to work at exercising our ethics, and learn how to do it consistently, come what may.

How to get Promoted

We have to learn from those who have not stuck to the values they say they hold, and the price paid for their moral failing. It's important to consider the costs they inflict on society writ large. The lack of business ethics is expensive in terms of our personal and collective health and wellbeing.

Learning from organizations like the Ford Motor Co., it's easy to see how leaders can create a culture of silence by rewarding it. This may be done inadvertently, without intent. But the lack of attention to performance systems that tacitly reward authentic transparency and shelter ethical truth produces unethical organizational cultures.

For example, millions of people were impacted by the Ford Pinto in 1971. Documents showed that the company knew the vehicle's design was flawed from the very start. But they still went ahead with production. In a rear-end collision, the fuel filler neck could separate and puncture the fuel tank, spraying fuel into the passenger compartment and igniting. In 1973, an internal memo revealed an annual forecast of how many deaths Ford should expect from the defect. The company decided it was cheaper to deal with each lawsuit, rather than fix the fatal flaw. Nine hundred people died. Leaders' unwillingness to care about safety impacted the firm's financial stability and its reputation for decades.

This didn't change Ford's way of doing business.

Other scandals followed.

The National Highway Traffic Safety Administration reported that Ford's automatic transmissions built between 1966 and 1980 were defective. Slipping from park into reverse caused some of the cars to roll backward after parking. Again, Ford chose not to correct the design flaw. After causing 777 accidents, including 259 injuries and 23 deaths, the company's response was to send out 23 million stickers to vehicle owners, reminding them to use the parking break. As you might expect, the death toll continued to rise.

Then there's the General Motors scandal.

General Motors' leaders and their employees knew their Cobalt model was flawed. In 2007, Chevy recalled 98,000 cars as a result of failing to meet federal safety standards. But what made this scandal so demonstratively horrific was the fact that the vehicle's faulty ignition switch caused the cars to shut off at speed, deactivating safety systems, which contributed to fatalities. Like many of these auto manufacturing scandals, GM knew about the defective part as early as 2004. But deciding it was too costly to fix, they delayed action.

Like it was going to go away?

Really?

In 2006, GM covered up the problem through deceitful practices (via serial number trickery). After 9 years and 13 deaths, the company issued 2.6 million recalls for the Cobalt and Pontiac G5.

But the story doesn't end there.

Slammed with a $10 billion civil suit, GM's lawyers argued that the deadly vehicles were manufactured by the old bankrupt GM. Therefore, the restructured corporation wasn't responsible. They pointed the finger at their former organization, as the death toll continued to rise.

These scandals are not just from American manufacturers.

Toyota lied about its cars having issues with unintended acceleration, ultimately paying the U.S. government $1.2 billion to avoid prosecution. After the auto manufacturers blamed the drivers, investigators learned that the company hid documents that showed the gas pedal assembly was at fault. Toyota admitted they misled the public and recalled 9.3 million vehicles worldwide.

The penultimate case is Volkswagen's "Dieselgate" scandal. In 2015, the world's largest automaker's reputation was ruined. Its diesel-powered cars knowingly used software that allowed the car to pass emissions testing, but then later, during normal driving, the automobile's emission control system would shut down. As a result, the diesel cars ended up polluting far more than other cars. Millions of angry customers demanded answers and compensation, and Volkswagen sales plummeted. Estimates suggested that the nefarious actions will cost the auto maker $14.7 billion in the U.S. alone.

When striving to understand how these situations can occur, investigators generally find that leaders and organizational members know about the unethical activities occurring. People working in engineering, product development, research, design, and manufacturing are typically aware of the problems.

A ubiquitous problem is...

Automotive industry leaders have shown a propensity to foster organizational cultures that endorse silence.

Additionally, leadership tends to prompt the use jargon. Management may reference adherence to their firm's ethics code, but words on paper often lack teeth.

For example, when deconstructing the organizational culture at Ford, researchers found that leadership encouraged employees to avoid using words like "wreck," "crash," or "fire" when speaking to consumers.

I can only imagine what terms employees used to describe such horrific issues caused by faulty

automobile parts. Maybe "challenge," "concern,"
"difficulty," "inconvenience"?

Those assigned to take customer hotline calls were literally trained to protect the firm. They knew if they didn't put the company's liability first, they wouldn't keep their jobs.

To sustain their employment and avoid retaliation, employees learned to keep their heads down and go along with the leadership-imposed cover-up. In so doing, workers gained their managers' trust, helping them attain raises, promotions, and potentially being rewarded with positions of greater responsibility.

When challenged about the fact that they had engaged in a cover-up, Ford blamed their lack of communication on the fact that they had been undergoing a reorganization process during that period. The explanation was that their restructuring efforts led to uncertainty about reporting channels and an overall lack of clarity.

Excuse me?

The job of a manager is to ensure communication.

All leadership is supposed to be ethical leadership.

When firms go through an organizational change effort, members may be uncertain about their role and where decision-making power resides. This suggests that a lack of clarity and potential confusion could expose the company to moral risk.

There is NO EXCUSE for a lack of ethics!

When a firm is undergoing change, it means leadership has to double down in their efforts to make ethical strength explicit in performance goals, throughout the firm.

This suggests that managers in the middle need to increase their focus on the importance of openness, foster transparency, and encourage organizational members to give voice to their values, bring forward ethical risks, and address even the smallest areas of moral concern.

There is NO EXCUSE for being unethical!

It's often a ruse for unbridled greed.

Management should not reward secrecy, nor should it cover up gaps in ethicality. Reinforcing silence has a way of commanding obedience. Management needs to conduct regularly scheduled forums where employees can openly discuss ethical challenges and potential ethical risks. Once concerns are identified, they are not swept under the carpet. They are given the attention and care they deserve, with corrective actions collectively developed and implemented.

Business is not about finding a way to grab short-term profits. It's about building the integrity you say you value into the products and services the firm offers and creating sustainable long-term success.

The vast majority of employees may have felt that they didn't have a choice. Most people do not have multiple employment options or large saving accounts. We cannot risk losing our jobs. From an employee perspective, rocking the boat may seem like an unwelcome and dangerous option.

> *If you put yourself into their shoes, most of us cannot afford to lose our jobs either. We all have rent and bills to pay and don't have an immediate back-up job waiting for us.*

The Ford employees who actually stepped up and questioned the performance of the DPS6 transmission were considered "naysayers" and were tacitly accused of corporate mutiny.[7] This gross contortion of commitment to customers and product quality, translated into "being a good team player," meant silence is best. This secrecy supported the group's overall progress and thereby increased the team's value and the firm's success.

Ethicists make the point that employees were facing issues that pitted the value of loyalty (to the firm and co-workers) against other values. More specifically, ethical ones.[8]

Dissent and whistleblowing were downgraded almost instantly when other social values superseded them as being more important. Instead of being viewed as a person of virtue with moral courage, speaking up against unethical activities was recast as a weakness.

> *While people want to speak up for the truth, no one wants to be seen as a "snitch" or a "rat."*

As we saw in this case, once you're into the scheme of denial, it's hard to turn back. As reported in the *Detroit Free Press*, one engineer described the situation like this: "...they got to this point in the product development cycle where Ford realized they passed the point of no return."[9]

If leaders don't actively and continuously pursue honest and open communication, it will cease to exist. You become lost in your own lies. When the style of management instills obedience, it stifles an ability to hear ethical concerns. It also tends to silence an employee's desire to give voice to their values. This harkens back to the findings of the classic Milgram studies.[10] The findings showed the powerful ability for those in authority to control others, leading people to obey orders that go against human morality, to the point of executing another person on command.

Explicit or implicit pressures to conform and keep your head down ultimately corrode the moral fiber of an organization. Management can suppress the desire to speak up and share the truth. When Ford engineers and product designers finally owned up to the fact that harms were occurring as a result of the vehicle's faulty transmission, the burden of silence had become overwhelming.[11]

How does this happen?

Breaking through the moral barrier didn't have to be this hard and take so long. Instead of reaffirming loyalty via silence, Ford could have leveraged the concept of pride in their product quality as a part of their organizational commitment. Management could have supported a shared desire for all employees to speak up about any and all concerns when any issues emerged. Leaders became disproportionately concerned about shareholder value, and they lost sight of how their profits were attained.

I am not pointing fingers.

We, as humans, are all capable of being unethical.

Remember that the variables of person, situation, and context signal ethical issue awareness, clarity, and understanding. Taking these together, we can form a path to achieve positive organizational ethics. But these factors may also be a crucible to motivate actions that circumvent the application of character strength. We are all capable of being unethical. Give us the right circumstances, and we can forget to focus on the value of ethics. But remember this:

A person is always a part of whatever situation they are in.

When you point a finger to someone or something outside yourself, three fingers point back to you!

Whatever you attribute wrong actions to (fear, greed, groupthink, laziness, or any other human weakness), realize that on some level, we're all a part of the problem. Therefore, we're all part of the solution as well.

We can see in this case how management's focus on profit prompted them to mask ethical issues and then fake success. It also shows how organizational members were complicit. Ethical problems, left unaddressed, can grow like a cancer. Sometimes slowly. Sometimes quickly. But always in an insidious way.

If you are not careful, you can become part of unethical patterns that seem benign, but shape who you are over time.

Strength #4: Ethical habits are shaped by your environment, including who you work with and for.

Notes

1 Tangney, J. P., Stuewig, J., & Mashek, D. J. (2007). What's moral about the self-conscious emotions. *The self-conscious emotions: Theory and research*, 21–37.
2 Homans, G. C. (1950). *The human group.* New York: Harcourt Brace.
3 Blau, P. M. (1977). *Inequality and heterogeneity.* New York: Free Press.
4 Cross, R., Rebele, R., & Grant, A. (January-February, 2016). Collaborative overload. *Harvard Business Review.* Downloaded from: https://hbr.org/2016/01/collaborative-overload.
5 Wright, L. (April 19, 2018). New survey explores the changing landscape of teamwork. *Microsoft 365.* Downloaded from: https://www.microsoft.com/en-us/microsoft-365/blog/2018/04/19/new-survey-explores-the-changing-landscape-of-teamwork/.
6 Ibid.
7 Wall Howard, P. (December 5, 2019). Ford workers break their silence on faulty transmission: 'Everybody knew." *Detroit Free Press.* Downloaded from: https://www.freep.com/in-depth/money/cars/ford/2019/12/05/ford-focus-fiesta-dps-6-transmission-problems/4243091002/
8 Sapienza, J. D. (October 8, 2019). 11 of History's most infamous automotive scandals. *Motor Biscuit.* Downloaded from: https://www.motorbiscuit.com/11-of-historys-most-infamous-automotive-scandals/.
9 Ibid.
10 McLeod, S. (2017). The Milgram shock experiment. *SimplyPsychology.* Downloaded from: https://www.simplypsychology.org/milgram.html.
11 Gallagher, B. (December 22, 2019). The psychology of Ford's Fiesta and Focus cover-up. *Ethical Systems.org.* Downloaded from: https://www.ethicalsystems.org/content/psychology-ford%E2%80%99s-fiesta-and-focus-cover.

5 R-E-S-P-E-C-T

Aretha Franklin's classic recording of "Respect" is an interesting story, one that reflects the ironies of ethics in business, in particular, the music industry.

Her declaration to command respect through the song's lyrics served as a battle cry for a generation, and for all who followed. It showed how a confident black woman knew she deserved respect and would

DOI: 10.4324/9780429324284-6

stand up and claim it. Demonstrating empowerment, she became a role model for those oppressed by dominant forces, regardless of gender, race, or political beliefs.[1]

> *But respect in terms of how she was treated as an artist?*
>
> *Very little, in terms of how she was paid for that recording.*

There is an irony to her story, because of the serious lack of ethics in how she was compensated for her work. Many of the ethical issues within the recording industry remain concerns to this day, so it's important to understand their background. In doing so, you will better understand the role you play in supporting fair wages and pay for artists.

Sock it to me!

The inspiration for the song "Respect" came from drummer Al Jackson. He was said to describe his thoughts about coming home after a road tour, and how he deserved respect when he returned.[2] Otis Redding picked up on this idea and wrote the song

"Respect" for Earl "Speedo" Sims and his band, the "Singing Demons." When the band never finalized its production, Redding decided to record it himself.

Sims, who was also Redding's road manager, claimed that the song was written collaboratively. Redding told him that he would get credit for the song, but he never did.

Redding's recording of "Respect" went on to achieve top single status in 1965. It was a breakthrough hit for the artist. But when Aretha Franklin first heard the song, she felt she could do something different with it.

And boy, did she!

While Redding didn't immediately take to her version, he eventually gave in. In 1967, when he sang the tune at the Monterey Pop Festival, he introduced the number by saying, "This next song, is a song that a girl took away from me. A good friend of mine. This girl, she just took the song. But I'm still going to do it anyway."[3]

Franklin's version flipped the gender of the lyrics, as she co-arranged it with her sisters Erma and Carolyn. She added what became the song's signature line: "R-E-S-P-E-C-T...find out what it means to me"[4] and brought in the background chant "*Sock it to me*," which later became a mantra for the 1960s.[5]

SOCK IT
TO ME !

Her version of "Respect" is considered one of the best songs of the R&B era, earning her two Grammy Awards in 1968 for *Best Rhythm & Blues Recording* and *Best Rhythm & Blues Solo Vocal Performance, Female.* In 2002, the Library of Congress honored Franklin's version by adding it to the National Recording Registry. It was placed number five on *Rolling Stone* magazine's list of *The 500 Greatest Songs of All Time.* Among other awards, it has been included in the list of *Songs of the Century* by the Recording Industry of America and the National Endowment for the Arts.

And yet, Redding's estate and the song's publishing company still make money off Franklin's recording, because none of the royalties ever went to Aretha.[6] While she earned fans around the world from her anthemic call to empowerment, she received nothing from decades of the song's play. Franklin's recording has aired over 7.4 million times on American radio stations alone.

This flaw within the copyright law in music has given Aretha's "Respect" additional meaning, serving as an anthem for musicians fighting for their rights.[7,8]

The real tune

Unfair and even corrupt practices in the radio and rec-ording business have been a part of the industry since its inception. During the 1950s, the term "payola" was introduced, referring to the practice of manufactur-ing a popular hit by paying for radio airtime play.[9]

More recently, 1999 to be specific, a new technology changed the game, reducing the rights of perform-ers in ways that could not have been imagined. Just like that, you didn't need a record or a CD, you could simply download the songs you wanted online. The convenience was phenomenal. The problem? A lot of folks didn't play fair.

They found ways to get the music for free.

It might seem like it's 'free' when you find ways to get music without paying for it, but it's actually stealing. Can you name a few songs you downloaded that you didn't pay for?

1. _____

2. _____

3. _____

   _____

The company Napster was the first on the scene to create widespread downloading. While it went bankrupt, shortly after it started up, the damage was done. The "Genie" was out of the bottle, and there was no shoving it back in. Downloading was easy, but millions of people weren't paying for what they played.

Have you ever thought about how artists earn a living?

Since the industry's inception, record executives typically ended up with the majority of profits in the financial deals. Sadly, as the distribution modalities changed radically in the digital age, the unfair advantage got worse. Cellist Zoë Keating caught the attention of *The New York Times*: "After her songs had been played more than 1.5 million times on Pandora over six months, she earned $1,652.74. On Spotify, 131,000 plays last year netted just $547.71, or an average of 0.42 cent a play."[10] Scott Timberg of Salon wrote that Keating earned six times as much from her iTunes song sales than she did from her music streaming.

The Cracker and Camper Van Beethoven lead, David Lowery, became a crusader for musicians' financial rights. One of his headlines sums up the unethicality and lack of equity in streaming arrangements: "My Song Got Played on Pandora 1 Million Times and All I Got Was $16.89."[11]

The lion's share of profits derived from the music we love does not go to the genius talent that creates it. Given how artists have been losing out, streaming music is now deemed to be unethical.[12] Gryffin Media explained listeners would have to stream a song 36,866 times a month for an artist to afford *ramen noodles.* When people bought albums and even mp3s, there was a glimmer of hope that musicians could earn a decent income on their sales.[13]

> *As it is now, musicians are basically giving their music away.*

Some artists, like country singer Lyle Lovett, understand the realities of this platform and make the best of it: "I've never made a dime from a record sale in the history of my record deal. I make a living going out and playing shows."[14] While Lovett accepts the problem, and has found a solution that works for him, for new artists, or those who don't have regularly scheduled or lucrative performances, it's a palpable and ongoing concerns.

We carry the burden of an old business model, one that directs at least 70% of the royalties to the record labels. These companies used to provide distribution

for the artists. But the entire game changed with technology. While the original system had plenty of ethical issues, add to it the use of YouTube and Spotify, now we have illegal downloaders as well. Why should artists give up the bulk of their royalties to a record label company when the value-add of these firms is limited and often questionable?

Why not shake this up?

Streaming companies could step in and become a direct distributor/label, like Netflix did with entertainment (producing its own original content), holding the property for the artist. Then artists wouldn't have to pay third-party labels. Another modified model might be similar to what Apple Music did when they paid Chance the Rapper $500,000 for a two-week exclusive. Firms like Apple Music could also offer VC support service to new artists in an entrepreneurial venture investment arrangement.

Moving beyond the ethicality of remuneration, let's turn to how you get your music and entertainment. Do you download this intangible property in a way that is law-abiding? Even if you don't like the law, or find it limited or dysfunctional, it's still "the law." Copyright laws are put into place to protect the rights of ownership and fair use. Laws are instruments of society. The problem is they don't necessarily protect everyone justly and equitably.

Laws are often passed for the wealthy to keep and enhance their wealth. The law does not equate to ethics. Many existing statutes stand to serve a few, which does not mean equality, justice, or freedom for everyone. With progressive movements for social justice and equity made loud and clear throughout the world (*Me Too, Black Lives Matter, Earth First, Gay Rights,* etc.), there is real hope for systemic change.

To date, however, many rights in business are still freedoms reserved for the wealthy to make more money.

That said, democracy is a means to give voice to our values. While imperfect, voting is one way to exercise our views in the free world. Civic engagement, playing an active role in the creation of government policies, is a vital duty toward preserving the health of our democratic freedoms.

Maintaining our involvement in government's role as a watchdog agency has never been more critical, as technology (and the ethical issues associated with it) infiltrates every aspect of our lives.

Changing the game

Big tech transformed how we go about doing everything. That meant we needed new laws and social norms to accompany this industry. Just as rules ascribed to the use of the horse and buggy had nothing to do with how we drive cars, tech products and services needed to be codified. The existing copyright laws did nothing to protect the owners of products like software, music, and entertainment online.

Staying with this example of music, lawmakers slowly realized that suing millions of people who downloaded music illegally was never going to happen. So, efforts were taken to sue a few people, as a

means to try to set an example, striving to modify behaviors more broadly. From that action, all that really changed was that now most people understood that downloading music and not paying for it was, in fact, illegal. But they kept doing it anyway!

Without real and meaningful punitive damages, lawsuits have no teeth.

In this case, when one of the defendants turned out to be a 12-year-old child, the tactics were viewed publicly as, well, silly. This news fostered the impression that the laws simply lacked credibility. Although there are subscription services, many firms have complained it's not a profitable enough business model. Mind you, not for the artists, for the service providers.

The epidemic of illegal file sharing carried on!

Ironically, stealing, in this context, has the dubious luxury of an altruistic naming convention, further endorsing the behavior on a tacit level. Like many other laws that people don't like, it becomes culturally acceptable, recast as an acceptable norm. While we've been talking about music, this is the exact same story for your organization. They have to pay for the products they download, like software. Your company probably buys a license that includes multiple users. But it's not legal for you to copy this software, either to share or to take home.

Copyright law recognizes that all intellectual works (programs, data, pictures, articles, books, etc.) are automatically covered by copyright unless it is explicitly noted to the contrary (e.g., Public Domain). That means that the owner of a copyright holds the exclusive right to reproduce and distribute the work. For software this means it is illegal to copy or distribute it, or its documentation, without the permission of

the copyright holder.[15] With so many people breaking the copyright laws, legislators had to revisit the
motives behind this situation and figure out how to
educate, redirect, regulate, and punish the millions
who download illegally.

Was that even possible?

Many people with otherwise healthy moral intuitions
fail to see copying and/or file-sharing as theft. If they
do it, they further endorse the behavior as being socially acceptable. Cognitive dissonance is at work.

We're not stealing...
we're renting it for free!

It might be generational, in that folks under 40 seem to consider downloading and streaming as uncontroversial—certainly not an unethical behavior.

It's just what everyone does.

But look at it this way, would you just take a car off a rental lot without paying for it?

Good luck with that.

In terms of the music industry, some are waking up to the unfair treatment of artists and creating new approaches that seek to fund them directly. An awareness of the ethical issues has led to new platforms like Patreon, vehicles that allow artists to be funded directly by their fans. While this is by no means a replacement for legislation, it is an acknowledgment by many that they have to pay for the content they value.[16]

The demand for access to a highly valued social commodity—music—has been triggered and facilitated by technology. We have found ourselves in the middle of an ethical dilemma, one at the epicenter of business and society.

This is when and where we need regulatory reform.

Does the music move you?

Movements to encourage reform initially launched social media campaigns helping to promote awareness and grassroots support (e.g., *I Respect Music* and *Content Creators Coalition*). While legislation was years in the making and slow to pass, in 2018 the Music Modernization Act (MMA) changed the rates and the way mechanical royalties are being paid to copyright owners. The MMA also overhauled how the statutory boards and courts regulate collective licensing in the U.S.[17] The MMA doesn't address many of the inequities in the music industry directly. But it's a step in the right direction.

While Franklin's efforts are still left without proper remuneration, we do see progress. Laws reflect the social boundaries we, as a society, believe to be important. If we value music, we should respect the artists who create and perform it.

Pay artists for their efforts!

Mind you, no one said that all laws and policies are ethical. Providing tax loopholes to big companies is legal, but is it right, fair, just, moral, or ethical? To make government and organizational policies work for us, they must be co-created. That means active participation from everyone.

Philosophers have something to say about music's ability to elevate the best in humankind.[18] Music compels us to feel, and these emotions can help shape our character, which, in turn, impacts how we live our lives. If music can even remotely encourage us to experience sentient moments that increase our capacity for empathy, then it plays a vital role in helping us build and exercise moral character. Pay for, borrow from your public library, or use "public domain" recordings to hear Erik Satie's *Gymnopedie No. 1*, Steven Price's *Our Planet*, Eminem's *Lose Yourself*, J. Cole's *Love Yourz*, or Miles Davis playing *Autumn Leaves*.

Given your age and music preferences, I'm confident that at least one of these pieces will move you to pause, think, and/or care more deeply about something or someone. Appreciating music helps us to value and respect one another, and the nature of what it means to be human.

Strength #5: If the rules are not working to ensure ethical behavior, get involved to help change them.

Notes

1 Brown, D. L. (August 16, 2018). How Aretha Franklin's 'Respect' because an anthem for civil rights and feminism. *The Washington Post*.

Downloaded from: https://www.washingtonpost.com/news/retropolis/wp/2018/08/14/how-aretha-franklins-respect-became-an-anthem-for-civil-rights-and-feminism/.

2 Black, J. (2008). *Classic tracks. Back to back singles.* San Diego, CA: Thunder Bay Press, p. 71.

3 Redding, O. (2014). Respect, "live" at the Monterey Pop Festival, 1967. Downloaded from: https://www.youtube.com/watch?v=7BDw-H_hUzw.

4 Sisario, B. (August 17, 2018). How Aretha Franklin's 'Respect' became a battle cry for musicians seeking royalties. The New York Times. Downloaded from: https://www.nytimes.com/2018/08/17/arts/aretha-franklin-respect-copyright.html?rref=collection%2Fsectioncollection%2Fbusiness.

5 *Urban Dictionary.* (April 26, 2020). Sock it to me. *Urban Dictionary.* Downloaded from: https://www.urbandictionary.com/define.php?term=Sock%20it%20to%20me.

6 Guiney, N. (May 19, 2014). Aretha Franklin, others deserve radio royalties. *The Boston Globe.* Downloaded from: https://www.bostonglobe.com/opinion/2014/05/18/radio-royalties-aretha-franklin-other-performers-deserve-piece/ccXkqbrseizNXMa5bHxdyH/story.html.

7 Nickels, W. G., McHugh, J. M., & McHugh, S. M. (August 21, 2018). Aretha Franklin's "Respect" and the fight for radio royalties. *Introbiz.TV: From the news to the classroom.* Downloaded from: http://introbiz.tv/aretha-franklins-respect-and-the-fight-for-radio-royalties/. See also (same authors), *Understanding business* (9th ed.). New York: McGraw-Hill Irwin.

8 Brown, D. L. (August 16, 2018). How Aretha Franklin's 'Respect' became an anthem for civil rights and feminism. *The Washington Post.* Downloaded from: https://www.washingtonpost.com/news/retropolis/wp/2018/08/14/how-aretha-franklins-respect-became-an-anthem-for-civil-rights-and-feminism/.

9 History.com. (April 26, 2020). This day in history, February 11, 1960: The payola scandal heats up. *H: History.* Downloaded from: https://www.history.com/this-day-in-history/the-payola-scandal-heats-up.

10 Sisario, B. (January 28, 1013). As music streaming grows, royalties slow to a trickle. *The New York Times.* Downloaded from: https://www.nytimes.com/2013/01/29/business/media/streaming-shakes-up-music-industrys-model-for-royalties.html.

11 Breihan, T. (November 12, 2013). Dave Lowery leads effort to shut down lyric websites like Rap Genius. *Stereogum.* Downloaded

from: https://www.stereogum.com/1562552/david-lowery-leads-effort-to-shut-down-lyric-websites-like-rap-genius/wheres-the-beef/.

12 Richmond, H. (November 14, 2014). The most ethical way to stream music: Not at all. *Center for Digital Ethics & Policy*. Downloaded from: https://www.digitalethics.org/essays/most-ethical-way-stream-music-not-all.

13 Ibid.

14 Herstand, A. (September 8, 2014). Fans aren't going to pay for music anymore. And that's OK. *Digital Music News*. Downloaded from: https://www.digitalmusicnews.com/2014/09/08/fans-arent-going-pay-music-anymore-thats-ok/.

15 *Washington University in St. Louis.* (April 26, 2020). Guide to legal and ethical use of software. Downloaded from: https://wustl.edu/about/compliance-policies/computers-internet-policies/legal-ethical-software-use/.

16 *Patreon.com.* (April 26, 2020). Creativity over everything. *Patreon.* Downloaded from: https://www.patreon.com/.

17 Flanagan, A. (September 19, 2018). A music industry peace treaty passes unanimously through Congress. NPR: Music News. Downloaded from: https://www.npr.org/2018/09/19/649611777/a-music-industry-peace-treaty-passes-unanimously-through-congress.

18 Cox, D., & Levine, M. (2016). Music and ethics: The very mildly interesting view. *Oxford Handbooks Online*, New York: Oxford University Press. doi:10.1093/oxfordhb/9780199935321.013.145m, 2016.

6 Money before morality

Corporations are a lot like people.

They reflect those who create and represent them.

It naturally follows that companies reflect the complexities and dualities of their human leaders. Just as we've all met the person who brags about their acts of charity while engaging in gossip behind another person's back, we often see businesses that say they care about integrity, but actually lack its sustained presence.

Like people, companies can have conflicting values.

Profiteering can be generated at the expense of others, while simultaneously the corporation donates to important causes that contribute to society. Working to establish ethical congruence requires a stakeholder approach.

That means money is earned in concert with respect toward people and the planet.

DOI: 10.4324/9780429324284-7

We must ensure that sentient beings and the natural environment benefit from business and are not destroyed by it. This requires thinking about **how** the organization's bottom line is actually achieved.

Corporate moral failings are often rooted in valuing short-term gains, demonstrated via metrics that target quarterly shareholder returns. This puts stakeholder considerations in jeopardy. Rather than embracing a Triple Bottom Line (TBL) approach (valuing people and the planet in how profits are established), the corporation focuses mainly on increasing its return on investment (ROI).

Building corporate ethics from character strengths—what the company does well, right, and good—is a means to achieving growth in a positive manner.[1] But sometimes we must look failure directly in the eye, in order to learn from it. If there is a genuine desire to change, leaders can purposively alter the motivations that supported past decisions, forming new choices that endorse ethical principals in how money is made.

If there is a desire to learn from mistakes, we can work to prevent them in the future.

The great hope for humanity is that something good can come from harms done in the past.

Why focus on Boeing?

The Boeing Corporation can serve as a learning platform to help us understand a range of business ethics issues. This includes a consideration of pay and benefits, discrimination, harassment, and equity, and the difference between stated and lived values in how goals are achieved. We will see how a targeted focus on profits erodes the moral core of a corporation and results in disastrous consequences for humanity.

Boeing embodies many of the challenges that organizations face when they adopt a traditional shareholder model. As a leading defense contractor, the company bears one of the most checkered ethical records in corporate history. By reflecting on their actions, we can see how a pattern of malfeasance stems from ethical incongruence.[2]

> *Einstein observed that doing the same thing over and over and expecting different results was the definition of insanity.*

Boeing has a history of contentious relations with unions and has often been accused of retaliating against them. A slew of contracting scandals in the 2000s forced the company's chief executive to resign and prompted Congress to strip the company of a $20 billion Pentagon deal (although it managed to get that contract award reinstated). Having worked for the company early in my career, I can also draw on some of my own experiences. These anecdotal narratives are used to highlight aspects of the firm's culture. As you read on, please bear in mind that:

✓ Boeing's ethical missteps are not uncommon among corporations.
✓ The company's actions are symptoms of deeply embedded issues that reside within the shareholder approach.
✓ The problem of moral myopia in business serves as a starting point for recognizing that systemic change is needed.
✓ If we do not alter the root cause of a problem, unethical outcomes are bound to return.

Behind the scenes (or how the sausage is made)

To start this process, we must look behind the scenes. So, let's think about this in terms of theater.

Have you ever been in or watched a play?

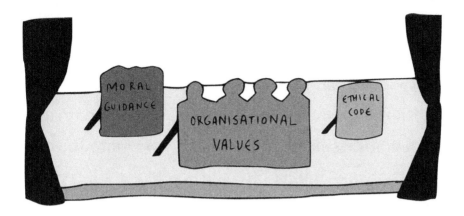

The stage is set to convince the audience that the narrative is real. Similarly, theatrical props are used to create an ethical image in business (it's called marketing). In theater and film, there's a startling difference between what is contrived in the camera lens and what is actually going on. I know firsthand by observing the process. I was cast as an extra in a movie starring Kevin Bacon, called *Telling Lies in America*. The awful irony of the movie's title is that we watched the tragic reality of this young co-star, Brad Renfro, struggle with behavioral issues on set (later attributed to his struggles with addiction).

What's on the stage or shown on camera is a very narrow controlled area. Backstage, the reality is much different. What looks lovely on the face of things can be downright nasty behind the scenes. To look at business ethics, we have to take down the facade, remove the window dressings, and discover the real truth.

When the ethical code, organizational values, and moral guidance are on pretty brochures, in the training modules, and presented elegantly on manicured websites, they seem real. But these words and images are not always lived, i.e., actually woven into the culture of organizational life.

> *Corporate ethics is not supposed to be just for show.*

> *When ethics becomes like theatrical staging, rather than actualized in how performance is achieved, we're in trouble.*

Most people like to believe in magic (even when they know it's a trick or mirage). Take, for example, the millions of guests that visit the Disney properties around the world annually. People enjoy pretending and using their imagination. The notion of play, in all its forms, serves an important role in fostering resiliency, creativity, and innovation.[3] But when impression management gets in the way of seeing and admitting the truth, it can be disastrous for business ethics.

> *It's not simple or easy to let go of the stories we tell ourselves about ourselves.*

We sometimes want to pretend that everything is wonderful, even behind the scenes. Intentionally mixing metaphors, it can be pretty gross seeing "how the sausage is made!" Nevertheless, we must look more closely at the truth behind the ethical issues that emerge, in order to learn from them.

To understand the Boeing story, it's important to go back to the company's beginnings. The organization was founded on the premise of making the impossible possible. Over 100 years ago (July 15, 1916), moving from a single canvas-and-wood airplane to transforming how we fly over oceans and into the stars, Boeing became one of America's most iconic companies.

As a beacon of innovation in corporate achievement, the firm predicated its success on imagination and creativity. The core principles were based on the idea that leveraging human drive, collaboration, teamwork, and design could be used to accomplish remarkable feats of engineering.

Landing the job

As a person who remains in awe of aeronautics, it's probably no surprise that when I moved to Seattle,

Washington in my early twenties, I was excited about the prospects of working for the Boeing Corporation.

I started off as a contracted worker, which, in those days, was explicitly defined as a temporary position. I was an office clerk pinch-hitter with part-time hours. The job had a start and end date. There was no full-time long-term work associated with temp hires. If I wanted a full-time job with benefits, it was up to me to figure out how to make that happen. Going beyond the dictates of my contracted temp duties, I created and self-directed an internal marketing project for myself. I wanted to learn everything I could about the company so I could become a valuable asset to the firm. Bear in mind, this was ancient times, when records were on paper.

I know, it seems impossible to imagine now!

Looking back, it was like a graduate research project on the history of marketing at Boeing. I read documents. I talked to people. I collected articles, brochures, conducted interviews, and wrote briefs about how projects were conducted. I asked questions. Then, I created a huge timeline on my office wall of the history of their marketing programs. Mind you, it was not a critical review; rather, a story about how the marketing program presented its aircraft. This caught the eye of the VP of Marketing. He thought it was a fabulous wealth of information that I had amassed, of my own volition. He was impressed. Shortly thereafter, I received an offer for a full-time position with a competitive salary and benefit package. As a Product Marketing Specialist, I was proud to be a part of a company with such a rich heritage and excited to wear the official Boeing badge.

The job "win" was bittersweet.

Within early days of my hire, I was asked to surrender my entire collection of marketing materials to the U.S. Department of Justice. I felt terrible, like I had done something wrong. But my new boss said not to feel bad about it; they were taking documents from everyone. Tons (literally) of papers were being seized from employees and transported to an airplane hangar for inspection.

It was a shocking experience.

I'll never forget how the joy of becoming a new employee had suddenly soured. Little did I know that the reason for the DOJ investigation was that Boeing's Marketing Department had a common practice of procuring classified Pentagon planning information to get a heads-up on their contracting proposals.[4,5]

> *I remember hearing people say, "Everyone does it; it's not that big of a deal."*

The stage was set. The corporation immediately presented itself as an organization with a conflicted moral identity. Now, think about where you work. Ask yourself:

> *Does my organization present conflicting values?*

> *Is my organization ethically congruent?*

> *Does my organization say one thing about its values and then engage in actions that are not in keeping with them?*

Given that the distinction between part- and full-time work relates to a timely ethical issue, let's examine this more closely.

Distorted compensation

The provision of benefits to employees, or the lack of doing so, has robust implications and consequences for everyone. In the U.S., contracted workers typically do not receive healthcare coverage. Since the 1980s, when I was at Boeing, many full-time positions in corporations all over the world have since been reclassified from full-time jobs to contracted roles. Globally, the so-called "temporary workforce" has grown exponentially. In the U.S., since the end of the Great Recession (2007–2009), the number of temp positions rose by more than 50% (roughly 2.7 million people).[6]

Firms now regularly hire part-timers to engage in full-time work.

This includes swapping job classifications so that employees are no longer benefits-eligible, which is tantamount to a massive compensation. It's a way for employers to decrease your compensation while looking like they still pay the same amount, because the base salary number has stayed the same. These kinds of actions have been great for the bottom line and the stock market. But they also reinforced the concept that benefits, like healthcare and a retirement pension, are no longer an employer's responsibility. In countries that have no social welfare programs (like the U.S.), this places the burden on individuals. Ultimately, this translates into many people going without healthcare, without savings, and having to live without a financial safety net. Corporations have externalized these costs to those who do not have the means to afford them.

Building a doc-in-the-box approach to medical care is not the solution.

An unintended consequence of having more and more contracted employees (people who are really full-time workers) is that we reinforce a lack of sustained commitment between the organization and its members.

This goes both ways.

Sure, a temporary contract-based system affords flexible hours, and people have the dubious luxury of job hopping. You can quit whenever you want, without bearing a sense of obligation. But this scheme results in many workers never having stability or the security of having set hours or a steady income.

We received a glimpse of just how many people are living paycheck to paycheck in the U.S., when unemployment skyrocketed during Covid-19 (in April 2020, 22 million people filed for government benefits).[7] Many multinational corporations and well-known brands strategically save on labor costs by using contracted full-time workers. Firms like FedEx, Amazon, General Motors, McDonald's, and PepsiCo buoy their profit margins on the backs of subcontractors, franchisees, vendors, and other part-timers. Midsize companies and smaller organizations claiming financial exigency terminated workers. Then they immediately turned around "cherry picking" a select few, hiring some back at reduced salaries, but without benefits.

This presents a complex crucible of issues.

Ethical concerns abound stemming from an array of reasons. This may include decisions driven by good intentions, but without considering the long-term implications and/or consequences of short-term thinking.

Should you care about this ethical concern?

If you do, what can you do about it?

In the U.S., we haven't figured out where the "benefit burden" should reside. In the meantime, many citizens go without basic healthcare and millions have no savings cushion.

You can be engaged.

Begin now!

We need to be aware of the systemic business ethical issues, think about them, and be responsible toward igniting positive change.

Being responsible means doing your best to demonstrate your values via the choices you make (where you work, the companies you choose to do business with, where you invest your money, etc.). You can begin by asking questions.

Is it the duty of the corporation to provide benefits to its employees?

To unpack these and other relevant ethical concerns, history sheds some light on how U.S. citizens became dependent upon employers for healthcare. Prior to socialized medical programs, healthcare benefits were either absent or philanthropically provided. During World War II, runaway inflation was a grave concern. To stave off this problem, the U.S. passed the 1942 Stabilization Act, designed to limit employers' ability to raise wages, and thus compete on the basis of pay for scarce workers.

Corporations began to offer benefits as incentives. In the 1950s, the unions effectively used their clout to pressure firms to increase these benefits. In time, costs escalated, and the promise of healthcare became unsustainable. Fewer people were paying into the system, people were living longer, and medical costs rose precipitously.

Bit by bit, through the combined forces of mismanagement, economic downturn, and fraud, employee benefits and healthcare programs were limited or simply trashed. For example, my husband's program with the Cleveland Water Department was cut, before he ever received a dime of it. The retirement healthcare benefits he paid into for over a decade were lost. After having socked away money for years, it went to zero with the stroke of an accounting adjustment.

I'm sorry, but that money you invested and the healthcare we promised you and your family— well, it's just gone.

This news has been emerging for decades, repeatedly. Commitments of employer benefits that were promised and contributed to were never delivered. Coming to terms with this unethical mess, the fact emerges that the U.S. needs to form some sort of partnership between employees, employers, and the government with an agreement of shared ownership for providing basic benefits like healthcare.

Some folks say, "Let's simply disconnect healthcare from work." OK. Let's do that. But that idea is predicated on the assumption that every business pays its workers enough so that they can afford to buy their own healthcare and that healthcare is genuinely affordable. Until we figure out how to do that, or some other solution, a cavern of inequity is exacerbated by political factions, spurring a lack of trust, and fanning a focus on short-termism. Complemented by economic policies that deregulate or manipulate pricing (e.g., on drugs), lobbyists can buoy government programs that benefit corporate interests at the expense of citizens.

Such actions continue to derail stakeholder considerations.

While my own Boeing job came with a good salary and benefits, after several years of working for them, I observed another aspect of this story. I noticed how some employees became dependent upon their ties to "the corporation"; it seemed to stifle their ambition. It was as though their life had become a *fait accompli.* They were locked in. Their destiny was cast, and they were just waiting for retirement, when they could begin to enjoy themselves.

I will never forget seeing a co-worker react to the receipt of his paycheck. Twice a month, like clockwork, he would announce the number of years, months, days, and minutes left until his retirement. While he said this with gleeful anticipation (as he daydreamed out loud about the fishing trips he would someday take, looking forward to a time when he would truly enjoy himself), it prompted noteworthy concerns in my mind.

What I remember (as a young adult) was telling myself, "Wow, I really have to figure out a way to earn a living where I'm not waiting to live my life." While a salary and benefits bring some level of security, if a job stifles your ability to continue to learn, grow, and enjoy your life, it can also mitigate your well-being.

What's more, you may begin to tolerate the unacceptable.

Watchdogs are still barking

As a Boeing employee, I experienced sexism and verbal abuse (both male- and female-sourced). Recalling that this was the 1980s, many human resource laws and employee protections had not yet been put into place. While there are still gender inequities when it comes to pay, position, and power, today's federal and state regulations in the U.S. now work to prevent these kinds of behaviors. In the twenty-first century, workers have the right not to be harassed or discriminated against because of age, race, ethnicity, national origin, sex, disability, or religion. More specifically, discrimination and harassment are defined as follows:

> **DISCRIMINATION** is when a member of a protected class receives unfair treatment based on being a member of that group. This might be denying a woman a promotion just because she is a woman. It is illegal because gender is a protected class under the law.

HARASSMENT is the pattern of behavior toward an employee that results in a discrimination
charge. Whether harassment takes the form of
verbal, physical, sexual, or other form—it is typically one of two types: quid pro quo ("give me a little kiss honey, and you'll do well here") or a hostile
environment ("I'd watch my back if I were you").[8]

While I'd like to think Boeing changed their ways,
decades later the company still shows up on human
resource watchdog reports (e.g., "EEOC Drops Hammer on Workplace Harassment").[9,10] The U.S. Equal
Employment Opportunity Commission enforces federal laws that make it illegal to discriminate against a
job applicant or an employee because of race, color, religion, sex (including pregnancy, gender identity, and
sexual orientation), national origin, age (40 or older),
disability, or genetic information. It is also illegal to
discriminate against someone if they complained
about discrimination, filed a charge of discrimination, or participated in an employment discrimination investigation or lawsuit.[11]

Equality at Boeing, as in many large corporations
during the 1980s, meant that the vast majority of

senior-level positions were equally shared by men. Today we see some improvement, with women now a part of Boeing's leadership team. But it still lacks balance. Of the 24 major leadership positions (including CEO/President, Executive Council, and other Corporate Leaders), 6 are held by women (roughly 22%).[12] Research has shown how women tend to be more relational, empathetic, and reflective in their decision-making efforts, which support moral choice-outcome paths.[13] Helping to achieve equity and ethics is certainly a substantial reason to maintain a gender balance on a corporate leadership team.

The inconceivable becomes reality

Regardless of how good of a person you think you are, it is important to remember that anyone can be corrupted by the behaviors of others. The preponderance of folks I worked with and for at Boeing were thoughtful and hard-working, with a commitment to their company, one that they dedicated their ingenuity to daily.

Part of my job was to take information to the men and women who worked in the wiring department. Delivering materials to them in the manufacturing hangers, I had a chance to see the intricacies of their efforts. At the time, wiring was especially hands-on. Many of their electrical tasks required an amazing attention to detail. It was almost impossible to imagine how all those wires could be configured in such an elegant maze of circuitry to accomplish the graceful feats of engineering that they were destined to perform. These people were dedicated, caring, thoughtful, and committed to the aircrafts' safety and quality. It was as though the planes being manufactured were literally an extension of those who built them, which in turn was an expression of the corporation's identity.

A brand is a fusion between the company, its employees, and the products and services they produce.

I recall a corporate roll-out party when thousands of employees came to the hangar to celebrate the launch of a new plane. Cheers, whistles, gratitude, and balloons flew up and converged in the air, representing a collective moment of shared success. It was an extraordinary gathering that was inclusive and energizing. Just writing about it gives me goosebumps, despite the many decades that have since passed. It was a party where everyone brought a little piece of themselves, which collectively contributed to something very special. You realized viscerally, in that moment, that you had become something far greater than yourself.

Since I left the company, and decades thereafter, Boeing's manufacturing line in Everett, Washington has continued to produce aircraft worthy of employees' corporate pride and respect. However, in 2019, this reputation for quality was severely damaged in the firm's myopic quest for profits. Given a lack of sustained care for quality, Boeing compromised the very heart of its operations and the soul of its organization. Boeing management risked the safety of its passengers, which ultimately took 346 human lives. As a result of executives focusing more on money than in how that money was being made, the company became embroiled in an ethical tragedy. The issue presented alarming news headlines. Excerpts from these stories provided shocking details:

- Massive layoff of 2,800 employees, as company halts production of the 737 Max jetliner.[14]
- Former President and CEO, Dennis Meulenberg, leader of the firm from 2015 to 2019, during the period when the 737 Max had its first flight, received FAA approval, and when the two fatal crashes occurred, leaves firm with $62.2 million in stock and pension awards.
- Investigatory documents showed how employees mocked federal rules, deceiving regulators, and joked about potential flaws, as the 737 Max was developed:

    "Would you put your family on a Max simulator trained aircraft? I wouldn't."

"I still haven't been forgiven by God for the cov-
ering up, what I did last year."

"This airplane is designed by clowns, who are in
turn supervised by monkeys."[15]

Linked to the causality of the crashes, pilots lacked
an understanding of how the plane worked and their
ability to take over manually. Tests evaluating the
new software during a post-crash assessment showed
that many of the pilots did not use the correct procedures to handle emergencies, but instead relied upon
their skills, which were apparently not in sync with
the plane's programming. Despite the loss of life, Boeing continued to argue with the FAA that simulator
training was not necessary.

Ongoing investigations revealed that employees knew about instances in which the company concealed information from government regulators.[16] After the plane's worldwide grounding, costing the firm billions of dollars, Boeing reversed its course and ceased production. In keeping with the industry's focus on profit, a Citi analyst noted, "This erodes one of the key selling points of the Max."[17]

"Safety is Boeing's top priority," stated Greg Smith, the firm's interim CEO.

Public, customer and stakeholder confidence in the 737 Max is critically important to us, and with that focus, Boeing has decided to recommend Max simulator training combined with computer-based training for all pilots prior to returning the Max safely to service.

Really?

I mean, REALLY?

I would say to Boeing, I believe you arrived at this conclusion because you had no choice. I don't think it's because you cared, first and foremost, about people's safety.

The firm's primary goal was to get more money to the bottom line faster.

Unless deep transformation occurs within the bedrock of a shareholder-driven firm and its associated organizational culture, profits remain at the top of the corporate values hierarchy. When you design and market a product via cutting corners so that you can sell more of them, safety is not a genuine, number-one priority, above all.

On January 7, 2021, it was officially announced that Boeing would pay $2.5 billion to resolve federal criminal charges regarding the 737 Max conspiracy, according to the U.S. Justice Department. The agency said Boeing admitted that two of its technical pilots deceived regulators about a software system that was implicated in both crashes. No amount will ever "resolve" this case for the families who will never see their loved ones again.[18]

Learning from Boeing, let's consider how safety and innovation must go hand in hand.

Running the morality train

Perhaps the Boeing tragedy can be our guide, to direct a future where we think about morality and the ethical issues that may emerge before an accident happens. For example, think about where we're heading with artificial intelligence (AI) in cars.[19] This has overtones of Professor Philippa Foot's classic "trolley problem," but with added complexity.[20]

The simplified version of this thought experiment prompts the reader/learner to decide on what to do, given the following information:

A runaway trolley (train) is moving at breakneck speed down the tracks. Just ahead, the track splits into two different paths. You are responsible for directing the train toward one of them. In one direction of the tracks, there are five people tied up and unable to move. The train is headed straight towards them. You are standing at a distance, managing the lever to guide the train's directional course. If you pull this lever, the train will switch to the alternate set of tracks. This path has only one person tied to the track and unable to move.

What is the right thing to do?

- Do nothing and allow the train to kill the five people on the main track.
- Pull the lever, diverting the train onto the other track where it will kill one person.

Explain your answer and justification below:

_____

_____

_____

This problem sets up a clash between several schools of moral thought.[21] For example, Utilitarianism, which considers the "consequences" of one's actions and Deontological ethics, which refers to "intentions" and "rights."[22] Deontology, also known as Kantianism, is driven by rules or moral laws to distinguish right from wrong. One could argue varying responses to the question from a host of alternative philosophies. Answers can be derived from slightly different reasoning in each examination. The results may be similar or different, in terms of what is determined to be a so-called "right" response.

How you make a decision matters.

Using just one moral philosophy is not enough.

It's important to run your problem though as many diverse perspectives as possible, and to look at the pros/cons of each. For good measure, always add in the virtue perspective, with prompts like:

What action would be the most compassionate and fair?

What response seems to be the best for the most people?

How do your values, moral identity, and character strengths help you determine your decision?

As with many ethical dilemmas, no matter what perspective you apply, you may not be given to know what is wholly "right." When you throw in unknown variables, things can get really messy. As new information is introduced, rational decision-making can take a back seat. Emotions often guide our sense-making, and without conscious awareness, they can inadvertently drive the bus! Many times our emotions steer our choices, without our navigation. Perhaps you opted to pull the lever and take one life over five. But what if that one person was your mother, husband, or your dog?

Yikes! That's a different story, right?

You most likely tossed out your prior analyses and said, "No way, I am not pulling the lever now!"

Understanding ethics means utilizing multiple philosophies and applying them collectively to determine what is your best "right" action given the current circumstances. This means we need to consider the people involved, the context, and the situation, and have as diverse a group as possible feeding into the process to give the most perspectives. But that does not mean one right solution. You obviously cannot consider variables that remain partially or totally unknown to you. Nor can you fully temper tacit beliefs that implicitly guide your judgment.

Biases steer our thinking without our even realizing it.

Consider too, that when we project the possible consequences, they are merely a best guess. A forecast, if you will. As time passes the solution may become less effective, inappropriate, outdated, or even unethical (yes, regardless of your original "good" intentions). It's tough to remember that what seems fine today may morph into a very bad idea indeed.

Like life itself, ethics can be a moving target.

Entrepreneurial innovation continually emerges from an amalgamation of known and unknown variables. Projecting how to proceed ethically demands deliberate reflective prudential judgment and the ability to adjust your thinking and strategy, as additional information is actively garnered.

Were Boeing leaders honest with themselves about how they were achieving the corporation's goals?

Did Boeing's management seek out information and adjust their strategy to ensure that the planes were designed for rigorous safety?

Were corners cut so that pilots didn't have to engage in costly training?

You can observe the complexities of ethical decision-making as you consider society's active interdependency on artificial intelligence (AI), particular in automobiles. How would your car choose between hitting a cyclist or swerving and taking a telephone pole head on? Such a choice may not be realistically derived by either a person or a machine in a split second.

But what if it were?

Could AI programming include empathy, mindfulness, shame, guilt, and pride in its decision-making effort? How would the choice be made? In whose best interest does the car act? Should it save you (the driver) or the cyclist? What if that choice was between saving you or five cyclists?

Whoa, that puts a whole new spin on things.

That's like the train scenario, only in reverse. Setting aside self-interest (I know, it's impossible, but try), what if AI in cars saves more lives, overall? But by the same token, it might cost some of the lives of people you know? When you study ethical scenarios, they might seem distant and not related to your own personal circumstances. But when you experience them firsthand, you realize that they are all around you in the fabric of your everyday life.

One March morning I merged onto California's highway, South 101. I no sooner got up to speed when the entire highway came to a full stop. I mean everyone was stopped. No inching.

NOTHING.

No movement for hours.

I couldn't imagine what the holdup was. Of course, a major accident. But were those involved OK? Did help arrive? Conversing with the drivers next to me in the complete standstill, we concluded it must be really "bad."

It was.

On the news that night we learned that a Tesla Model X had slammed into the divider. The driver lost his life. The accident was later linked with the car's semiautonomous autopilot system accelerating seconds before the fatal crash.[23] An additional problem at the scene was that the car was a threat to rescue workers, as lithium batteries have explosive properties. So, the accident site was treated like a potentially explosive bomb site.

Have we really thought through the health and safety implications of using batteries in cars?

Tesla argues that it has the safest car on the market. Some stakeholders disagree with that declaration.[24] The argument depends upon the metrics being used to determine and/or establish safety, which can vary by whoever conducts the study.[25] It's important to consider the source. For the information to be reliable, it needs to be an unbiased empirical study, which means it's not the company or a paid consulting firm performing the inquiry. Biases in what information is collected and how it is reported can shape the reported findings.

Much like the Boeing training issue, does autopilot mean you don't have to know how the car operates? How much knowledge does the driver need to operate the vehicle? What is the ethical intersection between the person and the car in decision-making? Do we need to know how to drive anymore? Most of the DMV test questions used to be simple and straightforward (except for the one about making a left turn on red). But with new capabilities of self-driving vehicles, we need to explicitly ask ourselves some very basic questions.

Just because we can do it, doesn't make it safe, honest, appropriate, just, good, or right.

Annexing this idea in general, i.e., the use of batteries in cars, have industry leaders and consumers considered how genuinely green their use will be over time? Few stakeholders are aware that mining lithium and disposing of it may, in fact, present even dirtier pollution issues than those produced by the internal combustion engine. The upshot is that the situation may be far worse than the problem the industry is purportedly moving to resolve. Again, this is a reflection of short-term capitalism and a lack of systemic thinking.

This also applies to how we go about our jobs and achieve our performance objectives. It may not be in your job description, but do you take the time to get more information when you're unsure, when something doesn't "look or smell right"? Do you think about the longer-term implications of your decisions before you take action?

We love fresh bread

In retrospect, what have we learned from Boeing? Do you question others (employees, managers, leaders) in your workplace about your concerns? Do you discuss with management and your co-workers about how performance is being achieved? What about how products are being made, sold, and marketed to your clients? Do you feel comfortable speaking up about issues that seem problematic, questionable, or could potentially present ethical risks?

How does your organization share information?

Think about how your CEO, managers, supervisors, co-workers, or team members communicate with you and each another. Recall several examples that relate to your organization's day-to-day operations and how people share or disseminate news. This might be scheduling details, job duties, instructions, or perhaps reports related to the health and welfare of organizational stakeholders. Consider the tone or style that was used in their delivery.

Reflecting upon these texts, emails, and/or letters, what was ineffective or effective about them? Was the information conveyed in a timely, thoughtful, and mindful manner? Was it inclusive or condescending in some way? Were the messages apathetic or energizing? Was the material presented in a clear and concise way, or was it confusing and disorganized? Sketch out a few examples:

1. _____

2. _____

3. _____

_____

Why were these messages particularly effective or, conversely, why did they fail to inform? It does not have to be either/or; it can be and usually is a bit of both. Reflect on the fact that you like to be informed, and in a way that encourages you to appreciate what is being shared. People value being informed and apprised as to what's going on. We all like to be "in the know."

Information is like bread.

We love it when it's fresh!

To get information, we often have to explicitly ask for it.

Do you regularly seek out and ask for more information?

Do you question things that don't seem right?

Do you make an effort to stay informed and ensure that others are included?

Do you seek to understand, learn, and share knowledge with others?

Would you rather be in the dark?

If we want information, we also have to be willing to give it.

Do you readily share information, or hold it close to your vest?

Would you prefer others not know what you're doing?

Does your company believe in and act with transparency?

Corporations, in their quest for profit, may cloak important information that is essential to life and well-being.

Two-faced

Boeing will be forever linked with an ethical disaster. But by the same token, the firm has actively demonstrated the capacity to do good. Boeing has always maintained their commitment to philanthropic generosity. In 2019, the firm exceeded $230 million in corporate gifts.[26] This included charitable giving, corporate contributions, employee giving, and employee gift matching. Employee giving has always been a strong component of the firm's culture.

In the 1980s, I served on the *Boeing Employees Good Neighbor Fund* (BEGNF) for my division. Working with Bill Gates Sr., the divisions of the firm joined forces to help our local community. Today, the firm's *Employees Community Fund* (ECF) continues to provide funding to projects that offer a variety of services. Employee contributions assist the homeless, supply food banks, and support at-risk children, while also providing job training for the unemployed and aiding veterans' programs.[27]

The paradox is that when the philanthropic arm of corporate-linked goodwill is separated from how its profits are achieved, organizations can simultaneously do good and cause harm. When a company embraces a shareholder approach, "doing good" may be bifurcated from how the organization achieves and measures its performance. This can result in a kind of split personality, a corporate identity that actually lacks integrity.

At some point, a lack of ethical congruency can provide an opening for moral slack (also known as greed).

This firm manufactured a product that put their passengers at risk, ultimately costing lives. In their myopic quest to garner profits, they failed to think about the implications of their strategy, and its potential to cause harm. Supporting good causes is wonderful. But such actions can never cancel out unethical corporate behaviors.

Boeing is not alone in this distinction.

A host of companies[28] have made it to the headlines for their failure to uphold their stated values. Ironically, you'll find some of these companies appearing on both the "worst" and "best" of corporate lists, in terms of their ethical performance.

Hey, wait a minute!

How can that be?

Well, in some aspects they are exceptional. In other areas, they not only miss basic ethical targets, they head south for an unethical finish. When you do not sustain your corporate integrity throughout your entire operations, you end up with a kind of wishy-washy ethicality, which will impact the organization's character, reputation, and profits. Boeing closed out the fourth quarter of 2019 down 37% from the fourth quarter of 2018. The company's net losses of $636 million for 2019 marked its first annual loss since 1997.[29]

A lack of ethics in business will eventually catch up with you, your organization, and the bottom line.

Table 6.1 provides unethical exemplars. News headlines that lead with an ethical scandal, targeting many well-known name brands, are sadly all too common. But it does not have to be this way.

Sometimes no amount of money can ever pay for harms done.

The loss of life can never be undone.

To describe the ethical issues associated with each of these firms would require several more volumes. But guess what? They bear an uncanny resemblance to Boeing's list of ethical issues.

The commonalities are unmistakable. Summing it up, we see consistent evidence of:

✓ Lying, cheating, stealing, and greed
✓ Sexual harassment, discrimination, and inequity
✓ Profit ahead of safety, integrity, and other basic principles
✓ Environmental degradation and/or disregard for life
✓ Lack of human rights and social justice

Table 6.1 Corporations Making News with Unethical Headlines

Amazon	Apple	Barclays
Bayer (Monsanto)	Cargill	CBS
Chevron	Coca Cola	Dow Chemical
DuPont	Equifax	Exxon
Facebook	FIFA	Ford Motor Co.
FoxConn Comm	General Motors	Johnson & Johnson
Kraft Heinz	Nestlé	Primark
Royal Dutch Shell	Tesco	Toyota
Turning Pharma	Uber	Union Carbide
United Airlines	Volkswagen	Walmart
Weinstein Co.	Wework	World Bank

I reserve hope that corporations like Boeing, and those who lead them, can produce meaningful and lasting strategic course correction. But it is doubtful that anything more than surface fixes will occur when the shareholder approach defines the organization and when the firm's ethicality remains consistently incongruent.

Boeing was back at it in 2020, once again appearing in the news with reports of their unethical maneuverings. *The Washington Post* headline states, "Boeing tried to amend bid after guidance from NASA official, raising concerns it received inside information."[30] Whether or not the allegations are true is yet to be determined. But given Boeing's track record, it seems like the same old story.

When nothing changes, nothing changes.

We must put our time, talent, and wallet share toward companies that put business ethics into motion. They are corporations that live the values they say they hold. They provide a safe workplace, offer fair pay and benefits in an environment free of harassment and discrimination, and ensure the well-being and care of employees, customers, and stakeholders (including the natural environment and all sentient beings).

Regardless of the magnitude of your daily decisions, they all have ethical elements and ethical consequences. Every choice you make and action you take requires your deliberate attention and care.

They all "count."

Please don't be asleep at the wheel of your life.

Like it or not, we are all impacted by the lack of business ethics. Sooner or later we all pay for its absence. So please, let's learn from mistakes that have been made. Help to ensure that history does not have to be repeated. Take charge of your choices and make business accountable for upholding ethics.

Strength #6: Make decisions with the knowledge that all life is precious, more important than profits.

Notes

1 Sekerka, L. E., Comer, D. R., & Godwin, L. N. (2014). Positive organizational ethics: Cultivating and sustaining moral performance. *Journal of Business Ethics*, 119(4), 435–444.
2 Mattera, P. (February 20, 2020). Boeing: Corporate rap sheet. Downloaded from: https://www.corp-research.org/boeing.
3 *The National Institute for Play.* (May 21, 2020). Opportunities: NIP, Carmel, CA. Downloaded from: http://www.nifplay.org/opportunities/.

4 Wilson, D. (January 14, 1990). 'The Fall Guy' speaks out – but convicted ex-Boeing official refuses to name sources. Downloaded from: https://archive.seattletimes.com/archive/?date=19900114&slug=1050689.

5 In 1989, Boeing pled guilty; a senior marketing analyst "took the fall" for the company and was sentenced to two years in prison. In an interview with the *Seattle Times*, he described how he was hired by a VP of Marketing to execute the task he was imprisoned for, which was a common practice in the defense industry.

6 Moran, A. (April 24, 2020). Employee extinction? The rise of contract, temp, workers in business. *Time Doctor*. Downloaded from: https://biz30.timedoctor.com/employee-extinction-the-rise-of-contract-temp-workers-in-business/.

7 Long, H., & Van Dam, A. (May 8, 2020). U.S. unemployment rate soars to 14.7 percent, the worst since the Depression era. *The Washington Post*. Downloaded from: ttps://www.washingtonpost.com/business/2020/05/08/april-2020-jobs-report/.

8 Gunter, N. (April 24, 2020). Harassment & discrimination at Work. *Learn How to Become*. Downloaded from: https://www.learnhowtobecome.org/career-resource-center/discrimination-and-harassment-in-the-workplace/.

9 Gurchiek, K. (August 10, 2018). EEOC drops hammer on workplace harassment. *SHRM*. Downloaded from: https://www.shrm.org/resourcesandtools/hr-topics/employee-relations/pages/eeoc-drops-hammer-on-workplace-harassment.aspx.

10 Ibid.

11 United States Employment Equal Opportunity Commission. (May 23, 2020). *Overview*. Downloaded from: https://www.eeoc.gov/overview.

12 Boeing (May 21, 2020). *Our company: Executive biographies*. Downloaded from: ttp://www.boeing.com/company/bios/index.page#/chairman-president-ceo.

13 Hoffman, J. J. (1998). Are women really more ethical than men? Maybe it depends on the situation. *Journal of Managerial Issues*, 60–73.

14 Gregg, A., & MacMillan, D. (January 10, 2020). Boeing's departing CEO leaves company with $62 million amid 737 Max supplier layoffs. *The Washington Post*. Downloaded from: https://www.washingtonpost.com/business/2020/01/10/airplane-fuselage-supplier-spirit-aerosystems-lays-off-2800-wichita-due-boeing-737-max-production-cut/?utm_campaign=news_alert_revere&utm_medium=email&utm_source=alert&wpisrc=al_business__alert-economy&wpmk=1.

15 Karloff, N. (January 9, 2020). Boeing employees mocked A.A.A. and 'clowns' who designed 737 Max. *The New York Times.* Downloaded from: https://www.nytimes.com/2020/01/09/business/boeing-737-messages.html?searchResultPosition=2.

16 Isidore, C., & Levitt, R. (January 10, 2020). 'Designed by clowns': Boeing releases flood of troubling internal documents related to 737 Max. *CNN Business.* Downloaded from: https://www.cnn.com/2020/01/09/business/boeing-documents/index.html.

17 Baker, S. (January 14, 2020). A Boeing employee called Lion Air, the airline in the first 737 Max crash, 'idiots' for asking to have its pilots trained in flying the plane. *Insider.* Downloaded from: http://static6.insider.com/boeing-737-max-employee-called-lion-air-idiots-training-request-2020-1.

18 Department of Justice, Office of Public Affairs (Thursday, January 7, 2021). Boeing charged with 737 Max fraud conspiracy and agrees to pay over $2.5 billion. Downloaded from: https://www.justice.gov/opa/pr/boeing-charged-737-max-fraud-conspiracy-and-agrees-pay-over-25-billion.

19 Lim, H. S. M., & Taeihagh, A. (2019). Algorithmic decision-making in AVs: Understanding ethical and technical concerns for smart cities. *Sustainability, 11,* 5791.

20 Foot, P. (1978). The problem of abortion and the doctrine of double effect. *Virtues and vices* (pp. 24–33). Oxford: Blackwell.

21 Clark, J. (April 24, 2020). How the trolley problem works. *How stuff works.* Downloaded from: https://people.howstuffworks.com/trolley-problem.htm.

22 Greene, J. (2016). Solving the trolley problem. *A companion to experimental philosophy* (pp. 175–178). Downloaded from: https://projects.iq.harvard.edu/files/mcl/files/greene-solvingtrolleyproblem-16.pdf.

23 Baker, D. (June 7, 2018). Tesla Model X accelerated seconds before Highway 101 crash, report finds. Downloaded from: https://www.sfchronicle.com/business/article/Tesla-Model-X-accelerated-seconds-before-Highway-12975702.php.

24 Baker, D. R. (June 7, 2018). Tesla Model X accelerated seconds before Highway 1010 crash, report finds. *San Francisco Chronicle.* Downloaded from: https://www.forbes.com/sites/bradtempleton/2019/10/25/teslas-3q-safety-numbers-show-improvement-but-continue-odd-wording/#48c4dfb77676.

25 Isidore, C. (August 7, 2019). U.S. told Tesla it can't call the Model 3 the safest care ever tested. Tesla won't budge. *CNN Business.* Downloaded

from: https://www.cnn.com/2019/08/07/business/tesla-model-3-safety/index.html.

26 Boeing.com. (December 3, 2019). Boeing to give $48 million in grants to more than 400 global charitable organizations. *Boeing.* Downloaded from: https://investors.boeing.com/investors/investor-news/press-release-details/2019/Boeing-to-Give-48-Million-in-Grants-to-More-Than-400-Global-Charitable-Organizations/default.aspx.

27 Boeing.com. (April 23, 2020). Community engagement. *Boeing.* Downloaded on May 17, 2020 from: https://www.boeing.com/principles/community-engagement.page#/seeking-support.

28 *Ethical Consumer.* (2020). Company profiles. Downloaded from: https://www.ethicalconsumer.org/company-profile/.

29 Gregg, A. (January 29, 2020). Losses from Max grounding continue as Boeing reports another dismal quarter. *The Washington Post.* Downloaded from: https://www.washingtonpost.com/business/2020/01/29/losses-max-grounding-continue-boeing-reports-another-dismal-quarter/?utm_campaign=wp_news_alert_revere&utm_medium=email&utm_source=alert&wpisrc+al_news__alert-economy--alert-national&wpmk=1.

30 Davenport, C. (June 20, 2020). Boeing tried to amend bid after guidance from NASA official, raising concerns it received inside information. *The Washington Post.* Downloaded from: https://www.washingtonpost.com/technology/2020/06/20/nasa-boeing-bid-probe/?pwapi_token=eyJoeXAiOiJKV1QiLCJhbGciOiJIUzI1NiJ9.eyJjb29raWVuYW1lIjoid3BfY3JoaWQiLCJpc3MiOiJDYXJoYSIsIm Nvb2tpZXZhbHVlIjoiNTk3YzExNWRhZGUoZTI2NTEoZDBkODAzIiwidGFnIjoid3BfbmV3c19hbGVyd F9yZXZlcmUiLCJjcmwiOiJodHRwczovL3d3dy53YXNoaW5ndG9ucG9zdC5jb2vdGVjaG5vbG9neS8yMDIwLzA2LzIwL25hc2EtYm9laW5nLWJpZC1wcm9iZS8_d3BtazoxJndwaXNyYz1hbF9idXNpbmVzc19fYWxlcnQtZWNvbm9teSotYWxlcnQtdGVjaCZ1fc291cmNlPWFsZXJ0JnVobV9tZWRpdW09ZW1haWwmdXRtX2NhbXBhaWduPXdwX25ld3NfYWxlcnRfcmV2ZXJlIn0.X1jARetaY7RNWsf6PGYFpNz32ONbuPlKoh1xHdThik4&utm_campaign=wp_news_alert_revere&utm_medium=email&utm_source=alert&wpisrc=al_business__alert-economy--alert-tech&wpmk=1.

7   Don't lie to me

We all lie.

And guess what? We do it all the time.

Whoa! Now that's a bit of sobering truth.

If we know this about ourselves, we can begin to address it.

DOI: 10.4324/9780429324284-8

But will we?

I mean, do we even want to frame lying as a concern, one that we need to address?

With today's culture reinforcing lying from so many directions, in so many ways, so much of the time, it's hard not to rationalize and even affirm its appropriateness. Unfounded statements that are informed by ignorance are becoming the norm. Why are we accepting half-truths as fact, letting lies fly around on media like hyperbolically fueled germs?

It's unmitigated laziness and a disregard for the value of truth.

Aside from not valuing the truth, people have found advantages to lying that serve them in the short-term. Note the focus on immediacy, rather than the long-term benefit. We've gotten used to it. We're spoiled, to the point of mistruths becoming an accepted habit.

Think about it.

I mean, really THINK about it.

Lies come in various forms.

Some of the most common types are omission, altering/restructuring, denial, minimization, and fabrication. I'll bet you never realized lying had so much spice and variety!

Let's take a closer look and see if you recognize any of these examples:

1. OMISSION

This means you left something out. A lie of omission is when relevant information is simply not included. It's a form of basic passive deception.

The lie: The project is nearly done.

PS: If we get that information from Sam, who, by the way, just resigned.

2. ALTERING/RESTRUCTURING

Then there's the art of restructuring. Here, the genuine context is distorted. You might say something with sarcasm, changing the characters or altering the scene.

The lie: The success of the project will increase corporate earnings by X%.

PS: Assuming our competitor rivals go bankrupt by this Thursday.

3. DENIAL

Denial is hard to detect, given it is a refusal to acknowledge the truth about something.

The lie: I gave this project my very best.
PS: Considering how boring it was and how unmotivated I am.

I'm not in denial!
I just refuse to believe it...

4. MINIMIZATION/EXAGGERATION

Minimization or exaggeration are two sides of the same coin. Look for reducing the effects of a mistake, fault, or impact of a decision you made. Conversely, you might represent the situation, product, or outcome as being greater, better, or more successful than it really was (or is).

The lie: Everyone contributed equally.

PS: That's just not true. You know you did the lion's share (or, conversely, little or nothing).

The lie: The impact of this intervention will send waves of positive appreciative change throughout the organization for years to come.

PS: OK, measure that.

5. FABRICATION

Then we have fabrication, which is just deliberately inventing a falsehood.

The lie: I got there early (or stayed late).

PS: Let's hope they don't check the security cameras anywhere.

Now you're familiar, in general, with several forms of lying. Perhaps you noticed that our examples might work in several categories. What's more, in some cases, one could argue that a lie might even have ethical or "right" motives behind it.

Before we get to exceptions, let's establish the truth first.

Think about your day at work. Upon reflection, do any of these popular lines ring a bell?[1]

I'm almost there.

It must have gone to spam.

It wasn't that expensive.

I forgot.

My phone died.

It's great to see you!

I read it.

I am really enjoying the work.

That makes sense.

I'm good (fine, no worries, no problem, etc.).

It's almost finished.

I know, I know! You get the idea.
  But now (truthfully), we're almost finished!

Perfect.

You're a wonderful boss!

Traffic was bad (there was an accident, I missed my train, etc.).

I love it (like, etc.).

Great work!

I'm booked (at that time, date, week, etc.).

Little cheats cost us a lot

Many of these responses are considered social conventions, even cordial niceties. Instead of lies, we just see them as courteous norms to hedge against negativity. Let's cover it up further and call it gratuitous fictions!

Sure Gary, Aliens took the files!

I think we need to look at the cost of this habit and look at the root cause. Why do we lie, aside from laziness? Maybe it's our own insecurity? Perhaps we want to belong?

Feeling a part of the group is critical for human beings.

Sometimes we lie because we're trying to mask our true feelings. It's so important to be "a part of," we lie or go along with a falsehood to establish that wonderful feeling of belongingness. When you mask your feelings to achieve a goal through lies, you are likely hindering the natural cues that will guide your moral behavior. Sentiments like shame, guilt, or embarrassment are important social self-conscious and/or moral sentiments that help steer you toward moral behavior. If we block or ignore these moral emotions, we thwart our own natural ability to be ethical.

The key is to always look honestly at your motives.

When we lie, what's the reason? Are we looking out for ourselves? Are we looking out for short-term interests? Or, are we thinking about others and the implications of what we say, and the longer-term repercussions of lying?

Do you even know that you're lying?

Are you even trying to be truthful?

If someone says, "How do I look?" and you reply, "Actually, you look trashed and your hair is weird," unless it's your sibling or a *very* special friend, it would be totally inappropriate and rude! In the workplace it would probably be altogether unethical. And, in some states in the U.S., such a comment might even be illegal.

Respect is paramount.

You can almost always find something to be truthful about that's also respectful. If not, it's better to say nothing. If what you're adding isn't kind, necessary, or true, it may be better to hold your tongue. If someone presses you, insisting upon an answer, I believe there are ways to tread gently without lying. If you deeply respect the people you work with and the environment you work in, honesty and trust should be values that are lived, not just statements in ethical code training materials. Our society, especially a culture driven by social media, has become exceptionally sloppy around the value of truth. Many assume if it's said, it must be true. We assume if we think it, it must be right.

That's an opinion, not truth.

It takes work to reveal the truth. You have to research the facts, discuss them with others, include diverse perspectives, and consider a variety of philosophies and frameworks. As norms shift over time, I sometimes wonder if we respect truth as a value today.

If you care about the value of truth, you have to continue to fight for it.

Truth isn't just passing along information. It's seeking out facts, it's discovery, and it's working with others to co-create understanding. It's also questioning our assumptions. Some of us tend to assume we are ethical without doing any personal inventory work or self-monitoring. My sense is that we, as a society, have forgotten about the importance of truth.

> *Could our habituated lying contribute to a society and business culture that doesn't value honesty?*

Maybe our phones and the anonymity of Facebook, Twitter, Instagram, and other online portals create norms that give license to lying (omit/restructure/exaggerate)? The ability to shape a pseudo or false identity, or to remain detached within a virtual environment, has provided both people and organizations with free reign to spew unguarded falsehood. These platforms tend to exacerbate negativity and, I would argue, more lying.

People lie on email more often than when they put pen to paper.[2] Given we don't even really "sign" documents in our own hand anymore, this does not bode well for the value of honesty as more and more of our life is conducted in virtual/online environments.

Duke University Psychologist Dan Ariely helps us unpack the truth about lies, and why we need to pay attention to the social value of honesty.[3] We intuitively carry around this belief that there are "good" and "bad" people out there. This platform clouds the way dishonesty actually works. He says that there are a lot of disastrous consequences that result from misunderstanding some basic realities behind lying.[4]

While most of us aren't psychopaths, everybody has the capacity to behave badly.

Ignoring this fact is expensive to business, and ultimately to everyone.

Turns out, we are all willing to cheat a little. But there are only a few of us who cheat a lot. Ariely calls this the "fudge factor." He prompts us to consider speeding, double-parking, taking a refill (one that's not free), skipping out a fare that's due, or stealing a tune.

Most of us will cheat a little.

Similarly, we all lie a bit.

There's a point at which most of us know and feel that a falsehood becomes wrong.

But here's the thing.

The cost of all those little cheaters put together far outweighs the cost of all the big evildoers.

This bears repeating.

All of our little lies cost more than the big whoppers, because there's so many of them! I'm sure that morsel of information was not lost on the creators of the hit HBO series, "Big Little Lies."

It's you and me, and everyone else, cheating every day. Adding up the expense of all those little lies turns out to be the BIG expense to firms and to society.

These costs come right back to you and me.

Take internal fraud and theft costs within companies, for example. That alone is around $600 billion a year![5] I assure you, such losses are passed right back onto the consumer. It doesn't come out of corporate profits (that's for darn sure!). That's why prices escalate, cartons get smaller, and we continue to pay more for less. You might also take issue with the fact that those who are making the rules cheat. Moreover, there are countless examples of people making salaries that exceed their worth. We've certainly seen executives pad their expenses and get "exceptions" to whatever they want, whenever they want it. Hence, the idea that rules have to be applied consistently, with no special exceptions, has become a crucial standard for organizational ethics.

Rules bend and break.

Companies need to set explicit rules that are clear. Then, they need to apply them across the board, to everyone, at every level, reliably. If ethics are important to business, you cannot have two sets of rules, one for employees and then another for management and corporate executives. That sort of hypocrisy breeds discontent, resentment, and unethical decision-making.

Leaders set the precedent for every organizational member's actions.

It's not that employees will typically go out of their way to be unethical. But if they see a lack of integrity from the top, they lose reason to care about demonstrating their moral identity in the workplace. Then it's particularly hard to make a case for it. If there are two sets of rules, the basis for the business ethics rests on a foundation of sand. This sets the stage for injustice and a lack of equity.

Organizational inequality breeds distrust and a lack of ethics.

This is fodder for corruption, greed, and systems that foster inequity and injustice. We need processes and practices that are agreed upon; then we all need to use and follow them. The organization's ethics platform needs to be reasonable and viable, while it helps to guide employees' ethical decision-making. In short, it's knowing the rules, but also knowing how to apply your values as you work to address the ethics with every decision you make.

This notion of "doing the right thing" can be vague. Therefore, it's critical that how employees are expected to go about achieving their goals "ethically" is made explicit. Management needs to create and

nurture a "speak-up" culture.[6] Fostering this kind of environment is supported by managers:

✓ Walking their talk (role-modeling ethical discourse/discussion)

✓ Holding frequent sessions where ethical discussions are valued exchanges among teams and cross-functional groups

✓ Establishing performance metrics that honor both individual and collective achievement

✓ Providing anonymous reporting that is reliable and trustworthy, and leveraging this information to develop corrective actions to advance improvements

✓ Helping employees feel valued and ensuring that their contributions are recognized as vital elements of the organization's success

A lack of clarity and forthright application of "the rules" enables employees to justify doing what's right for them, nudging rationalizations that weaken ethics. People can end up excusing little lies, telling themselves things like:

I deserve this.

It won't count.

No one will notice.

Everyone's doing it.

They don't pay me enough as it is.

I'm Robin Hood! It's taking from the rich to give to the poor.

Just this once...

A lack of openness and transparency fosters righteous justification. Rationalization often fuels actions that are likely to serve one's own short-term interests, rather than the interests of others. Toward that end, it's important to eliminate conflicts of interest and a lack of clarity whenever and wherever possible.

The culture of the organization influences the ethical vibe of the place. It's the sense employees experience at work—what it's like to be at the organization as tasks are accomplished. If people feel that they're being treated fairly, they are more inclined to treat others in kind. When people are not treated fairly and sense that they're being cheated, disrespected, or undervalued, it breeds similar behaviors and retaliatory vengeance as well.

Corruption festers when inappropriate activities go unaddressed and employees begin to give up. Attitudes like, "Everybody is doing it" and "Who cares?" reaffirm ethical apathy. However, those with a strong moral identity may have the courage to continue to give voice to their values.

Authentic leadership is ethical behavior by example.

OK, so that's not exactly big news. You knew that already. But listen to this:

Ethical leadership is a state of mind.

Appoint yourself as the CEO of yourself. Regardless of your position at work, you're in charge of your own moral identity. That means being your best self, by way of example to yourself.

Honesty is a practice.

Business ethics takes a sustained effort.

Integrity is the quality of being honest and having strong moral principles. Having moral principles means using them!

Not as a matter of convenience, but as a matter of ingrained habit.

The people I know who are consistently ethical, individuals who taught me how to role-model honesty from within, continue to exercise their ethics. One never completes the job and finishes becoming one's best self. For people who are admirable, it may not have been a task that came easily. It has taken sustained personal commitment. Ethical people continue to strive to do the right thing, because that's who they are and who they want to be in the world. Regardless of an issue's magnitude, ethics is something they take very seriously.

> *Ethicality is a choice within every decision you make.*

Being honest isn't just when it's easy or convenient, or when it's visible to others. Integrity shows up as a real strength when no one will even see or know the difference.

> *You are truthful because it matters to you.*

The paradox of integrity in business is that, almost by definition, transactional dealings tend to encourage concealment and exaggeration. Experts on team performance have found that how people are compensated influences their ethicality—more specifically, how often they tell lies. One study showed that lying is more pronounced when there are team incentives to perform, as compared to individual pay-based incentives.[7] People tend to lie more under team incentives because they can diffuse responsibility. Deceptive acts can be deflected from the self to an outside source in an ambiguous manner. For example, when explaining the team's performance to your boss, a member might say, "If the supply chain guys had been on the ball, we would have been able to increase our sales this quarter by 20%."

Studies have also shown that younger males measuring high on the personality traits of extroversion

(E) and neuroticism (N) tend to lie more frequently.[8] Now, add in people who love to take risks and enjoy competition (both male and female) and you have identified the potential for workplace maverickism![9] This gives you a clearer picture of why putting business and ethics together is so hard. It's not impossible. But it's certainly challenging.

Those who are attracted to business and are good at it are the very same people who are most likely to lie and cheat.

Say what?

This does not mean it's impossible. What it means is if you want to see business ethics, you have to make a continual decision to ensure it's what you stand for and what you do. Not just when you feel like it, but on a daily basis. Entrepreneurs enjoy taking chances. Competitive business players want to win, score, succeed, and beat the odds to create wealth.

But do they want to do so ethically?

Mavericks tend to find their way into management, executive leadership, sales/marketing, human resource, and public relations positions.[10,11] And those working in business, on the whole, tend to be less ethical than people in other fields.[12]

Hmmm.

This is a serious problem.

Those attracted to business tend to have traits that do not support ethicality.

So just how do we exercise integrity in business, when the players are not prone to ethicality by nature? In a world where lying can be a bridge to getting the job done and helps us navigate the challenges (and hassles) of organizational life, how do we manage ourselves and each other to support honesty? Begin by finding how deep you're in. Examine your own thoughts and actions. Do a rigorous self-assessment.

Perform an HONEST inquiry into how often
you lie.

Make a sincere attempt to verify something as being reasonably accurate, not just citing something you heard on social media, or a morsel of gossip you picked up over lunch. It means cross-checking what you say and do, to ascertain the facts. Take a week—heck, a day will do—to get honest with yourself about where you shave the truth, exaggerate, or just blatantly tell a falsehood. Refer to the beginning of this chapter and consider the various forms of lying.

Think about each time you lie.

This can be leaving out information, embellishing the facts, creating social fictions, cheating, and so forth. You get the idea. Write down three examples.

1. _____

2. _____

3. _____

   _____

After completing this task, my business students typ-ically return to class summarily surprised by their blatant lack of integrity. Even those who score high in honesty on the VIA Character Strengths instrument[13] openly admit that they were caught off-guard when they realize how many lies they found themselves lob-bing throughout the course of a single day. While say-ing "I'm on my way," "It's almost finished," and "I only had a few" seem to be some of the most popular lies among Millennials, we all have mistruths embedded within and throughout our days.

I'm sure I watch more TV than I am likely to report.

I feel a twinge of guilt and/or shame in saying I watch an hour or so each night (that seems like a lot to me). Given my own perceptions, I now feel like I need to immediately justify that statement by saying, "it's only the news" or "it helps me fall asleep."

Who cares?

Why would sharing simple truths make us feel "less than" acceptable, to those around us? Sometimes not telling the truth reveals our insecurities. Exaggeration or puffery is a false path to establish self-esteem.

Forget the BS.

Just get real.

Be honest with yourself about your own lack of honesty. Take a bite out of morality and start exercising your moral identity.

Look in the mirror

Most of us want to be better, not worse, than whatever we are. I would guess we all want to be seen as right, good, and/or socially apropos. Comparing myself to others can be useful. That is, if it's helping me improve, accomplish something, do good for others, and so forth. But if comparative efforts drive

judgment, they can foster inappropriate criticism and create a fertile ground for dishonesty and unfair judgments. I might unconsciously be degrading the value of ethics in my life and in the lives of those around me. This can absolutely impact behavior in the workplace.

Norms get shaped by what we do and say.

Building character is about getting honest with yourself. It's important to feel the moral emotions of shame, guilt, and embarrassment when you're not being honest (and feeling pride when you come clean). Such feelings are meant to keep your morals in check! So, use them as tools to your own advantage. Social self-conscious or moral sentiments are natural cues that steer us toward right thinking and right acting in social contexts. The trouble here is that we like to avoid them. Rather than seeing them as assets, to bolster our moral identity, we tend to squelch them, thereby hindering their efficacy. You might also think, "So what's wrong with being optimistic about myself, embellishing my strengths and downplaying my weaknesses?"

It's not "wrong," per se.

The problem is that we get into habits of curbing corners. We soften the edges and round out truths about our genuine self. This practice becomes one of crossing the line (over to BS) as the norm. It's gotten to the point where many people don't even notice any more.

Take another look at yourself.

Why *are you lying about whatever you're lying about?*

To feel better about yourself?

To effectively compete and win?

To feel a sense of belonging?

To gain status or control?

To avoid feeling "less than" others?

Thinking about business, we make promises to our co-workers, customers, and other stakeholders.

Do we intend to keep those promises?

Can we keep them?

You've probably had the dubious chore of having to call your phone, cable, and/or Internet service provider because of a billing problem.

Am I right?

Recently I spoke to several customer service representatives at Xfinity as a result of my service going out and an error on the bill. I was promised several adjustments to my next bill, including a 20% credit for the inconvenience of having to call about the issues. Not only was the next bill wrong, the credits were *in absentia*. I then had to call again, to explain that the original problem was ongoing and that the credits were missing. I argued for yet an additional inconvenience credit for the additional waste of my time and energy for having to babysit the bill (which had not been right for four consecutive months). Companies regularly make promises to their stakeholders and do NOT deliver on them.

Wide-scale lying is pervasive.

That doesn't make it right. But on some level, I suppose it continues because people find benefit in continuing the habit. Lying does offer short-term benefits.

It gives us permission to get something (time, money, prestige, power, etc.).

We've all been ripped off, shorted, or scammed.

Maybe we deserve something extra this time?

Maybe the lie gets someone off our back?

Perhaps we're insecure and want to gain an edge?

Every time a lie is tossed into the system, we are systematically degrading the value of honesty. We help to normalize falsehoods, making the next lie easier and less noticeable. Lying lessens the value of honesty in our culture writ large.

While we have all had customer service issues, sometimes the consumer is the problem. Knowing someone who struggles on the front lines of a Customer Service Department for a manufacturing company, she explained how people constantly try to take advantage of her organization.

For example, having no proof of identity and yet demanding discounts. The company graciously created a program to offer price reductions to first responder and healthcare workers (during the pandemic). She described the exhausting nature of how people lie to

get these discounts, falsely claiming to be someone they're not. Given the company sells luxury items, it's not like they "need" the items.

A colleague and former executive of the Target Corporation explained how he had to let some employees go, when they decided to steal from the company. Sometimes they offered twisted excuses in their defense—like it was an attempt to reappropriate the wealth of the corporation elsewhere, as though they were "Robin Hood." Or, "It wasn't money I stole, just merchandise." At every level, embezzlement is an ongoing problem at Target, and throughout the retail industry.

Telling yourself it's OK to do something doesn't make it so.

Sometimes companies want consumers to believe something, so they just keep saying it over and over again.[14] People get used to hearing it and start to believe it's true, without even thinking about it.

Yes, even if it's a lie.

But it doesn't have to be this way!

Some leaders have decided to make their organizations work at being truthful in how they go about making money.

A "corporate promise" is like a normal promise, but we might break it at anytime!

Those making Ethisphere's *World's Most Ethical Companies* list have outperformed large-cap sector firms for the last five years by 14.4%.[15]

Table 7.1 Ethical Organizations: Ethisphere Examples (2019)

Company	Employees	Country	Industry
APTIV	150,000	U.K.	Automotive
Bimbo	138,000	Mexico	Food processing & distribution
BMO	45,454	Canada	Banking
Capgemini	211,300	France	Consulting services
Cementos Progreso	3,600	Guatemala	Construction
Conner	1,000	Hong Kong	Sourcing services
DTGO	800	Thailand	Real estate
EDP	12,000	Portugal	Energy/utilities
Elekta	3,700	Sweden	Medical devices
Illy	1,290	Italy	Food/beverage/ agriculture
Johnson Controls	120,000	Ireland	Industrial/ manufacturing
Natura	6,300	Brazil	Health & beauty
Nokia	100,000	Finland	Telecommunication
Orlen	24,113	Poland	Oil/gas/renewables
T-Mobile	217,000	Germany	Telecommunication
Wipro	170,000	India	Information Technologies

Table 7.1 outlines a few exemplars. Their criteria to judge business ethics include an evaluation of five specific areas:

1. Ethics and Compliance Program
2. Culture of Ethics
3. Corporate Citizenship and Responsibility
4. Governance
5. Leadership and Reputation

These firms illustrate that good things do come to those who engage in ethical business practices.

Playing a long-term game

It's worth taking a look at the firms appearing on their annual list, as it includes a wide range of organizations, from a vast array of sectors (50 in all).[16] Some of these firms employ over a quarter of a million people and are publicly traded (e.g., PepsiCo), while others are smaller, cooperatively owned and operated organizations (e.g., Teachers Mutual Bank). It is also important to note that these firms hail from all over the world, wide-ranging in their form, size, and type.[17] The industries extend well beyond those noted in the table, including but not limited to healthcare, financial services, insurance, machinery, environmental services, engineering and design services, aerospace, water and sewage, and retail.

Looking at the corporate ethics documents and training materials in corporations (ethical or otherwise), undoubtedly, the word "transparency" is mentioned. For transparency to be genuine, however, the organization does not hide or conceal the truth.

We have integrity.

We are transparent.

These statements cannot come with tacit caveats, like "when it's convenient," "when it's required by law," "when we're boxed into a corner," "when it looks good for us," "when we're in trouble," and so forth. Integrity and transparency require consistent openness with what the business is doing and how it goes about achieving its performance goals. It's about being honest, which is telling the truth about how you're conducting business. Without a doubt, trust is an essential element of any firm's stock and trade, literally and figuratively.

Ruth Cotter serves as the Senior Vice President of Worldwide Marketing, Human Resources, and Investor Relations at Advanced Micro Devices, Inc. Speaking to a group of business students about leading with ethics, she described a technique she learned from her father as a young girl. "Take a few minutes and give yourself a good look in the mirror. What do you see? Who are you inside?" She explains how this is an effective practice for keeping yourself in check. Being honest with others starts with being honest with yourself.

Honesty is at the very core of trust.

Without trust, there's no integrity.

Strength #7: If you value honesty, quit lying.

Notes

1 Daniel, A. (March 13, 2020). The 40 lies everyone tells on a daily basis. *BestLife*. Downloaded from: https://bestlifeonline.com/the-40-things-people-lie-about-most-often/.

2 Naquin, C. E., Kurtzberg, T. R., & Belkin, L. Y. (2010). The finer points of lying online: E-mail versus pen and paper. *Journal of Applied Psychology, 95(2)*, 387. Downloaded from: https://www.researchgate.net/publication/41967730_The_Finer_Points_of_Lying_Online_E-Mail_Versus_Pen_and_Paper.

3 Clark, D. (October 28, 2013). Dan Ariely on why we're all a little dishonest – and what to do about it. *Forbes*. Downloaded from: https://www.forbes.com/sites/dorieclark/2013/10/29/dan-ariely-on-why-were-all-a-little-dishonest-and-what-to-do-about-it/#682d6eb86579.

4 Ariely, D. (2012). *The (honest) truth about dishonesty*. New York: Harper Collins Publishers.

5 Zetter, K. (February 7, 2009). TED: Dan Ariely on why we cheat. *WIRED*. Downloaded from: https://www.wired.com/2009/02/ted-1/.

6 Ethics & Compliance Initiative (ECI). (December, 2018). Interpersonal misconduct in the workplace. *Global Business Ethics Survey: ECI*. Downloaded from: https://43wli92bfqd835mbif2ms9qz-wpengine.netdna-ssl.com/wp-content/uploads/2019/01/Global_Business_Ethics_Survey_2018_Q4_Final.pdf.

7 Conrads, J., Irlenbusch, B., Rilke, R. M., & Walkowitz, G. (2013). Lying and team incentives. *Journal of Economic Psychology, 34*, 1–7. Downloaded from: file:///C:/Users/Leslie%20Sekerka/Downloads/Conrads,%20Irlenbusch,%20Rilke,%20Walkowitz%20-%20Lying%20and%20Team%20Incentives.pdf.

8 Elaad, E., & Reizer, A. (2015). Personality correlates of the self-assessed abilities to tell and detect lies, tell truths, and believe others. *Journal of Individual Differences, 36(3)*, 163–169.

9 Gardiner, E., & Jackson, C. J. (2012). Workplace mavericks: How personality and risk-taking propensity predicts maverickism. *British Journal of Psychology, 103(4)*, 497–519.

10 Harper, H. (April 10, 2018). Is there a perfect career fit for your personality? *Workstyle*. Downloaded from: https://www.workstyle.io/career-choice-based-on-personality.

11 Lounsbury, J. W., Smith, R. M., Levy, J. J., Leong, F. T., & Gibson, L. W. (2009). Personality characteristics of business majors as defined

by the big five and narrow personality traits. *Journal of Education for Business, 84*(4), 200–205.

12 Mudrack, P. E., Bloodgood, J. M., & Turnley, W. H. (2012). Some ethical implications of individual competitiveness. *Journal of Business Ethics, 108*(3), 347–359. Downloaded from: https://link.springer.com/article/10.1007/s10551-011-1094-4.

13 For more information visit VIA Character at: https://www.viacharacter.org/survey/account/register.

14 Ryan, L. (June 29, 2016). The truth about Business lies. *Forbes*. Downloaded from: https://www.forbes.com/sites/lizryan/2015/06/29/the-truth-about-business-lies/#7c784ab71b8d.

15 Industry Week. (February 26, 2019). Being ethical has its perks: World's most ethical companies. *Industry Week*. Downloaded from: https://www.industryweek.com/leadership/companies-executives/article/22027217/being-ethical-has-its-perks-worlds-most-ethical-companies.

16 Ethisphere. (April 25, 2020). The 2020 world's most ethical companies: Honoree list. *Ethisphere.com*. Downloaded from: chttps://www.worldsmostethicalcompanies.com/honorees/?fwp_number_of_employees=0.00%2C469000.00.

17 Ibid.

8 Trust us

Take a U.S. dollar bill out of your wallet. If you don't have one available, simply look up the image. The words "IN GOD WE TRUST" are printed on it. For those reading who do not believe in God, do you value this currency? If a document bears a message that isn't true for you personally, is it suddenly worthless?

If you're an atheist, I highly doubt you'd refuse
an offer of one hundred-dollar bills (testing
out my theory).

Regardless of one's personal beliefs, society has agreed to use the dollar bill as a form of shared currency. We trust that it works as a mutually agreed upon document of value, even if we disagree with what's printed on it. The basis of trust is predicated on one's starting assumptions, defining the terms of use, and coming

DOI: 10.4324/9780429324284-9

to some form of agreement on what they mean and how they will be applied.

>*How do we establish trust when our views differ?*

This presents an interesting ethical dilemma. Case in point, the U.S. dollar bill. We use it as a form of exchange, even if we might not agree with what it declares. We are willing to overlook cognitive incongruencies because we value what the currency does for us, serving as a convenience in trade.

>*Can you imagine trading goods or providing services in kind, every time you went to the gas station or grocery store?*

I can picture myself asking some clerk if they would like a lecture on business ethics in exchange for some milk, bread, and a tank of gas. I don't think that would go over very well.

>*Now that I'm thinking about it, they might give me the stuff to get me to leave!*

Given the country's history, it's ironic that American currency references anything at all about religion.

Many came to this country to flee religious persecution. The freedom of religious belief was solidified in the first amendment to the U.S. Constitution. It states that "Congress shall make no law respecting an establishment of religion or prohibiting the free exercise thereof."[1] Alas, politics prompted the motivation to put the word "GOD" on the U.S. dollar bill as a means of Cold War propaganda.

This illustrates a major point: we don't all have to believe in what the dollar says on it to trust the fact that it has worth and we trust it to work for us. On any given day a dollar might buy a bottle of water, a senior coffee at McDonald's, postage on a first-class letter (1 oz.), an iTune, or .77 worth of British Pounds Sterling (along with any number of items at your local Dollar Store). The vast majority of people never worry about what this document has printed on it, because they rely upon the fact that, collectively, it offers buying power and helps us establish economic growth.

New vehicles for exchange have jumped into the mix, now representing currency in digital form. Apple-Pay, Paypal, and Venmo have emerged as monetary transactional platforms. Rather than emanating from governments, business has stepped in to foster the exchange of money for goods, shares, or services in an instant. If you want to discuss Dogecoin, Meme, or the many cryptocurrencies bombarding the market today, call Elon Musk (or conversely, watch him on SNL).[2]

Bear in mind, these transactions do not come with government back guarantees.

Why do you think these companies explicitly state that they are "designed for payments between friends and people who know and trust one another?"

Trust is an essential element for business to function.

We trust capital to work for us in business, as a resource. The same can be said of people. Money works on the basis of trust, similar to relationships.

Do other people know they can trust you?

Trust typically emerges over time. It suggests that others can rely upon you to be forthright and honest. Does your currency—your brand—represent worth, rendering the trust of people? It's hard to build trust. It's even harder to regain it once lost.

Consider AT&T, a brand once known for customer care. It is a company now on the compliance experts' watch list for becoming the next Wells Fargo.[3] It likes to sing its own praises for "living true" to its values. Yet simultaneously it continuously engages in unethical and/or questionable practices including upselling, setting up fake accounts, bill padding, and making payments that smack of bribery to government officials.[4,5] AT&T was required to pay $60 million, as a settlement deal for unethical throttling practices and barred from marketing plans that present speed or amount of data without full disclosure of specific restrictions.[6] Living your values doesn't mean you have prizes and awards. American essayist Ralph Waldo Emerson warned us of such actors when he wrote, "The more he spoke of his honor, the more we counted our spoons."[7]

We can be responsible in our efforts or become slack. A reliable work ethic earns us a reputation of dependability, one that engenders the value of trust.

Should other people (and the organizations they represent) want to invest in you, your brand?

To cultivate the value of your own brand, people need to have faith in who you are, what you can do, and what you bring to the table. Building trust is constructing a bridge toward executing the value you bring to business. Like the dollar, people must have faith in your ability to help them achieve their business goals. Truth and value are inextricably intertwined in forging relational trust.

How do you establish and build trust?

To answer this question, start by reflecting on examples from your own life. List three people that you can be truly honest with:

1. _____

2. _____

3. _____

_____

Maybe one of your confidants is a family member. Or it might be someone you've shared an experience with, like accomplishing a major project, achieving a difficult goal, or going on an adventurous trip. Perhaps this is a teammate, friend, mentor, colleague, or leader in your field or industry.

Of the people you listed, what do you consider special, unique, about them?

What sets them apart from others?

We often build trust through interdependence. Trust can be developed through hard times, when you've leaned into the strengths of others and they've been there for you, i.e., "had your back." Sharing tough experiences can foster resilience and build strength. But they can also forge a kind of faith, a belief in a person's genuineness of character. Spend some time thinking about those you identified in the thought exercise above. What makes them trustworthy? List reasons why these people, in particular, came to mind:

1. _____
2. _____
3. _____
   _____

We often trust people because they are reliably "good." We can count on them to care for us when we need it most. Trust holds us together. But for trust to function in a healthy manner, it must be predicated on truth.

The value of truth

Dissect any business ethics scandal and you'll find at its root a lack of truth. This is the crux of the business ethics oxymoron conundrum.

How do you encourage truth in business?

Scholars have examined human behavior for centuries, offering elegant theories and research studies to help explain and understand human response-actions. And yet, we keep making the same mistakes over and over again. Concepts like groupthink, fear of angering the boss, cognitive dissonance, and a host of other traps are well-known human psychological barriers that trick our better selves from taking charge. Some of this can be explained by group dynamics. Because the workplace depends upon teamwork, we have radically increased the propensity for ethical concerns to emerge.

A demonstrative example shocked Americans, and the world, when NASA's Space Shuttle Challenger and its courageous crew were lost, moments after liftoff. In 1986, all of the astronauts perished in this disaster before our very eyes. Nearly 20% of the American population simultaneously witnessed the horrifying

launch on live television. The presence of Christa McAuliffe as a member of the crew was particularly compelling to the nation, as she would have been the first teacher in space.

This disaster could have been avoided, had management been willing to listen to the truth.

At the time, Roger Boisjoly was a booster rocket engineer, working as a contractor for Morton Thiokol. He and four colleagues became embroiled in the fatal decision to launch the NASA Space Shuttle Challenger.[8]

Decades later, his account has become a well-known case study, helping business students understand how, when, and why good-intentioned people make irrational or non-optimal decisions. With pressure to launch the mission, there was an urge to conform and discouragement of dissent to speak up. In hindsight, no one wanted to cause a delay in the launch. Their work environment made the goal of hitting the target date so important that they became blind to taking safety precautions. NASA proceeded with the launch, despite the fact that engineers were aware of the risks in doing so (given weather-related issues).

Data revealed that the shuttle's booster rockets would not seal properly in cold temperatures. With unexpected freezing temperatures on the morning of scheduled liftoff, engineers (including Boisjoly) knew this launch was a tragedy waiting to happen. Just a few years ago, Bob Ebling, another engineer on the team, looked back on the disaster and said, "They had their mind set on going up and proving to the world they were right, and they knew what they were doing. But they didn't."[9]

A presidential commission studied what happened on that fateful day. They found flaws in the space agency's decision-making process. We have since become mindful of the dangers of groupthink. NASA has since altered their policies to prevent future disasters. But they were reticent to embrace change within their organizational culture. NASA leaders demonstrated difficulty in learning to listen to those beneath them. They knew about the engineers' concerns yet forced the launch despite their ardent warnings. When speaking truth to power is not valued, employees (regardless of the organization or industry) have a harder time escalating ethical risks and bringing forward issues that could hinder plans, schedules, and targeted goal accomplishment. Management may look down upon or turn against those who give voice to ethics. People who step up to the plate and share the truth about ethical issues demonstrate moral courage. In general, we look to those who blow the whistle about unethical activities as truth-seekers. If we want trust to exist in the workplace, information needs to be shared and openly discussed. Trust has to be the basis for business if ethics is genuinely valued.

We need each other.

Business is about building and sustaining relationships.

A friend and colleague of mine, Dr Tracey Messer, is a professor at Case Western Reserve University specializing in entrepreneurship and organizational behavior. She reminds me that "Everything in life is about relationships." Indeed, we are social beings. Dependence on, and cooperation with, other humans has enhanced our ability to survive.[10] Although societal conditions have changed, we still have the need to affiliate. Survival of our species depends on trusting and supportive relationships.

This is also true of business.

Developing, winning, and keeping customers hinges on establishing and building trust with others. Unfortunately, competing values can get in the way, like wanting to increase profits.

Money is both a want and need.

We all have wants and needs. We work hard to GET some things (achieve, attain, procure, etc.) and to AVOID others (evade, dodge, circumvent, etc.). Along the way virtue and vice influence our path. Ian Dury thought he summed up the latter when he claimed in his song lyric that human vice could be reduced to *sex, drugs, and rock and roll.*[11] All of these activities certainly show up in the workplace![12]

> *Please don't ask me about how one person described his/her workplace ethical issue as "people photocopying their butts."*
>
> *I swear, I don't make this stuff up.*

Unfortunately, Jeffrey Toobin, formerly of the New Yorker magazine, didn't get a chance to read this chapter. After indecently exposing himself on a staff Zoom call, the lead reporter was sacked. Toobin apologized for his actions. He stated he didn't realize he was visible on Zoom.[13]

> *Excuse me, pleasuring yourself during a staff meeting?*
>
> *If you're that bored, maybe staff meetings aren't needed.*

Along with the basic human desires, let's throw in money, power, status, the need to belong, and to feel

a sense of accomplishment. Additionally, you don't want to be disliked, ostracized, ridiculed, or to be cut out of the action. Loads of competing values there!

For many of us, today's workplace is entirely a social production. An organization is a communal activity. Whether it's face to face, on the telephone, through emails, or via Zoom, we work together to accomplish our tasks. As such, it's generally in our best interest to get along, and perhaps, even go along with the group.

Do you see where I'm heading with this?

The problem is that our values compete for supremacy. One of them usually ends up with top billing. When that occurs, a particular core value can take precedence over all of the others. I'd like to think we can do it all (values-wise). You know, get the job done, have time with family, give service, work out, take care of the house/laundry/meals/errands, and so on and so forth—all at the same time.

Is that too much to ask?

Well yes, it is.

Accomplishing everything, living all of my values, is not exactly how life rolls. Just as in business, it turns out that in many decisions, contexts, or circumstances, one value will win out. I relish compromises. I like it when everyone gets some of the prize. I don't like being forced into either/or choices with binary conditions. It's great when outcomes can be forged to become a "both/and" type of solution. But that's not how business typically works. Here, values compete for priority. You'll find situations when resources are finite and "something has to give."

At some point, you ultimately have to make value choices.

Harvard University Business Ethics Professor Joseph Badaracco calls these defining moments or "right versus right" decisions.[14] Personal and work values are often pitted against one another. The trick here is to not let these choices get into your face without planning for their arrival. If there needs to be a value choice, be present for it. Don't let your value choices be unconsciously determined. Or, worse yet, slug you! Make your M.O. (Latin, *modus operandi*, i.e., method of operation) one that's deliberate and purposeful. If you are led to a situation where you are forced to compromise your values, be open and clear about it (with yourself and others).

Should I spend time with my family tonight or continue to work?

Should I hold the project back to cross-check the numbers or rush to meet the deadline?

Should I hire more people or put the added duties on those already employed?

Defending your moral identity

Competing values will vie for supremacy. At the end of the day, a particular value can sneak up on you and claim the prize, sometimes at the expense of all others. This can be very costly to your moral identity.

Aaron Beam, a former CFO, shares his experience in this regard. As part of the $2.8 billion accounting scandal at HealthSouth,[15] he went to prison for the role he played in it. Becoming swept up in the trappings of money, prestige, and power that quick wealth offers, he lost a hold of his principles. In sharing his story to business students and executives today, Aaron doesn't mitigate his culpability. Rather, he presents his experience as a cautionary tale.

When the firm's stock soared from its IPO price of $6.50 to well over $20 a share in just a few short months, he was instantly worth millions. He built a large home, bought a condo in New Orleans' French Quarter, and purchased multiple luxury cars. Dropping $30,000 on Hermes ties on a New York City trip, he dressed the part of an investment banker who had "arrived." He liked being treated like a "rock star," receiving luxury accommodations and flying all over the world in a fleet of private jets. "I was greedy," he explains. Aaron got caught up in the charade of self.

Aaron was blinded by the money and had gotten so far into the scheme that when he considered pulling back, he felt he couldn't. He waited for the axe to fall.

It did.

On March 19, 2003, the NBC Nightly News led with a story about suspicions of an ethics scandal at Health-South. "At that moment I knew I'd probably be in prison in the not-too-distant future," Aaron explains to eagerly listening students today. After serving time in a federal penitentiary, Aaron now helps those in business learn from his mistakes. At a certain point, if something is not right, you have to defend and deploy your moral identity.

Your moral identity has to be lifted to the top of that values hierarchy.

When we let our moral identity go by the wayside, it's no longer a value we stand by. Dishonesty then has a fertile environment in which to grow. Striving to understand how dishonesty is cultivated in organizational settings, Ron Carucci, an executive coach and leadership expert, studies workplace behavior. He is interested in the role organizations play in steering members toward or away from honesty.[16] In hoping to help avert reputation and financial disasters that

dishonesty can lead to, he has found several factors, the first of which is the lack of strategic clarity.

The strategic plan provides a company with a roadmap for employees. It outlines where they are heading and how they're supposed to get there. If people don't have this map, they tend to improvise along the way. For example, employees who are unaware of or kept in the dark might say:

Who knows what's happening; we make it up as we go.

We're flying by the seat of our pants.

Yeah, it's like we're grasping at straws.

I lay low and just keep my head down.

Is the organization saying one thing and doing another? Employees know if their firm isn't "walking its talk."

In large part it's because they do a lot of the walking!

If there's deception, the organization is going against what it says it believes in. In such cases, employees will, at some point, follow suit. If there's uncertainty, people will fill in the empty spaces with whatever's handy. And that's usually what's convenient, not necessarily what's ethical. To build trust in the workplace, employees need information. If I'm expected to be a representative of my organization's mission, I need to know what that means explicitly, and how to achieve it.

In studying organizational honesty, scientists, using surveys, found that even modest increases of clarity (10%), represented by a shared and accurate understanding of the organization's strategic aspirations, improve employee truth-telling behavior by 5%. Along with a lack of information, lying in the workplace also stems from poor governance. When there's no respected process that brings key decision-makers together, enabling them to hold honest conversations around tough issues, the truth melts and trust can go right along with it. In an era when bullying has become a leadership style, we need to recall that negotiations are central to trust. Working collaboratively to discuss terms means to co-create a mutually acceptable outcome or goal.

Trust is central in order for any kind of productive and cooperative relationship to exist. When there is no trust, there is no effective process to prompt organizational members and key decision-makers to engage in honest conversations. Truth goes underground, leaving the organization to rely on rumors and gossip for news. Use of a system of governance can help set expectations for open dialogue. Its functionality, however, is predicated on the fact that management embraces truth and welcomes dissenting ideas.

When microclimates emerge, like departmental silos (clustered tribal-type groups within a firm), they're an obstacle to honesty. When conflict within an organization and/or between departments goes unaddressed, research shows that organizations are roughly six times more likely to have people withhold or distort information. Fragmentation, especially across divisional lines, creates dueling truths, resulting in one side having to prove they are right, and the other wrong. Divisional loyalties paint those who are outside the team as "the other," those to be blamed, feared, resented, or ostracized. Cross-departmental tensions can lead to an integrity disaster.

> *If you've worked in an organization where departments beef with one another, I need say no more.*

Susan, we are worried your department has become siloed

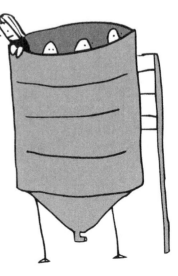

This doesn't help anyone in the long run.

> *Lying won't help you, your team, or your company.*

Dishonesty degrades the value of your personal and organizational moral identity. A lack of trust destroys reputations.

Leaders drive the ethical bus

People lie when they're incentivized to do so. We need to create performance metrics that encourage quality products and services, as well as ethical decision-making and behavior. This means paying people for manifesting the organization's stated values in how they go about doing their jobs.

In conducting their research, Accenture found that over half the firms they studied showed a measurable drop in trust when the company experienced a product recall, fraud, data breaches, or C-suite missteps, equating to a tune of at least $180 billion in missed revenues.[17]

But that's only part of the story.

Following that drop in trust, revenue growth continued to be negatively impacted, with a further downward drop of 10% (on average). Point being, it's expensive to lose stakeholder trust. It may or may not bounce back quickly. It can be a costly gamble.

Trust is not only good for a company's culture and its employees, but it also builds shareholder value. Ethical firms cultivate a culture of integrity. This is an organization where employees are comfortable speaking up, view leadership as trustworthy, and take personal ownership in making sure their company is an ethical place to work.

> *You want employees to take pride in the reputation of their firm.*

Research has shown that employees who give their CEOs high marks for character work for firms that have an average return on assets of 9.35% over a two-year period. That's nearly five times as much as firms with CEOs judged by employees to be low on character, according to Fred Kiel, the author of *Return on Character.*[18]

CEOs reflecting a lack of morality are identified as being highly self-focused. Their concerns are largely for personal gain and caring for themselves and their own financial gain. Conversely, when CEOs demonstrate integrity, responsibility, forgiveness, and compassion, they are identified with behaviors like standing up for what is right, expressing concern for the common good, recognizing mistakes (but not holding grudges), and showing empathy.[19] IBM is recognized as one of the world's most ethical organizations. CEO Gini Rometty, who now leads the century-old firm, explains, "We know our clients and the consumers they serve expect more than groundbreaking innovation and expertise. They want to work with a partner they trust, and one that works to make the world better, safer and smarter."[20]

Businesses around the world are showing they can step up to advance social development. By addressing issues like diversity and inclusion, firms not only support the letter of the law, but they also advance efforts to advocate and protect human rights, and the spirit behind it. Take, for example, Milliken & Company. CEO Halsey M. Cook says that business ethics is all about how you conduct your business. It's not just hitting your targets, but how profits are achieved. At Sony Corporation, CEO Kenichiro Yoshida says, "We know that ethical practices matter to our customers, our communities and our associates."[21] The company's operating with integrity and sincerity is central to the firm's identity, as much as its spirit of innovation.

A company's strategy ultimately has to be translated into its vision, mission, objectives, and values. Values must then be integrated into every organizational member's workplace experience. If there's a disconnect, the vision is not known or lived, ethics becomes inconsistent and what the company supposedly stands for doesn't show up in how the work gets done. This contributes to an environment of distrust. Working in such conditions, employees will follow suit: they too will withhold information or distort the truth. Trust empowers ethical decision-making and increases employee loyalty. What's more, trust decreases stress levels and hostility in the work environment.

You have worked hard. You are poised to accomplish whatever you set out to achieve in life. Make sure your goals are effectively realized by being diligent and purposeful about building trust, which depends upon your being consistently ethical. You have important work to do and it can be successfully delivered when you have built a trustworthy reputation.

Strength #8: Trust is a valuable commodity and the basis of lasting and productive relationships in business.

Notes

1 Cornell Law School. (April 25, 2020). U.S. constitution: First amendment. Cornell Law School, Legal Information Institute. Downloaded from: https://www.law.cornell.edu/constitution/first_amendment.

2 Akhtar, A. (May 8, 2021). Elon Musk calls the meme-crypto Dogecoin the 'future of currency,' predicts it will 'take over the world' on 'SNL'. *BusinessInsider.com*. Downloaded from: https://www.businessinsider.com/snl-elon-musk-dogecoin-hustle-future-currency-2021-5.

3 Jaeger, J. (October 15, 2019). AT&T might be the next Wells Fargo (and doesn't seem to be doing anything about it). *Compliance Week*. Downloaded from: https://www.complianceweek.com/boards-and-shareholders/atandt-might-be-the-next-wells-fargo-and-doesnt-seem-to-be-doing-anything-about-it/27872.article.

4 Sandler, R. (June 25, 2020). 'It Was Sell At All Costs': How AT&T's Sales Staff Created Fake Accounts For DirecTV Now. *Forbes*. Downloaded from: https://www.forbes.com/sites/rachelsandler/2020/06/25/it-was-sell-at-all-costs-how-atts-sales-staff-created-fake-accounts-for-directtv-now/?sh=6527ba2771ab.

5 Leiber, L. (May 10, 2018). AT&T gets ethics award and three hours later the company gets tied to Michael Cohen's money mess. *Dallas News*. Downloaded from: https://www.dallasnews.com/news/watchdog/2018/05/11/att-wins-ethics-award-and-three-hours-later-the-company-gets-tied-to-michael-cohens-money-mess/.

6 Kelly, M. (November 5, 2019). AT&T fined $60 million for throttling 'unlimited' data plans. *The Verge*. Downloaded from: https://www.theverge.com/2019/11/5/20949850/att-fine-unlimited-data-plan-fake-throttling.

7 Emerson, R. W. (1859). *The complete works of Ralph Waldo Emerson: The conduct of life* [Vol. 6]. Boston, MA: Houghton Mifflin Co/Riverside Press Cambridge.

8 Berkes, H. (February 6, 2012). Remembering Roger Boisjoly: He tried to stop Shuttle Challenger launch. NPR: The Two-Way. Downloaded from: https://www.npr.org/sections/thetwo-way/2012/02/06/146490064/remembering-roger-boisjoly-he-tried-to-stop-shuttle-challenger-launch.

9 Berkes, H. (January 28, 2016). 30 Years after explosion, Challenger engineer still blames himself. NPR: The Two-Way. Downloaded from: https://www.npr.org/sections/thetwo-way/2016/01/28/464744781/30-years-after-disaster-challenger-engineer-still-blames-himself#.

10 Sreenivasan, S., & Weinberger, L. E. (December 14, 2016). Why we need each other. *Psychology Today*. Downloaded from: https://www.psychologytoday.com/us/blog/emotional-nourishment/201612/why-we-need-each-other.

11 IMDb: Sex & Drugs & Rock & Roll, Ian Dury. (2010). *IMDb*. Director Mat Whitecross, writer Paul Viragh, cast/crew Serkis, et al. Downloaded from: https://www.imdb.com/title/tt1393020/.

12 Gutek, B. A. (1985). *Sex and the workplace*. San Francisco, CA: Jossey-Bass, p. 46.

13 BBC News. (November 14, 2020). New Yorker fires Jeffrey Toobin for exposing himself on Zoom. Downloaded from: https://www.bbc.com/news/world-us-canada-54912610.

14 Badaracco, J. (1997). *Defining moments: When managers must choose between right and right*. Boston, MA: HBS Press.

15 McCann, D. (March 27, 2017). Two CFOs Tell a Tale of Fraud at Health-South. *CFO*. Downloaded from: https://www.cfo.com/fraud/2017/03/two-cfos-tell-tale-fraud-healthsouth/.

16 Carucci, R. (February 15, 2019). 4 ways lying becomes the norm at a company. *Harvard Business Review*. Downloaded from: https://hbr.org/2019/02/4-ways-lying-becomes-the-norm-at-a-company.

17 Lyman, M. (October 30, 2018). The bottom line on trust. *Accenture Strategy Research Report*. Downloaded from: https://www.accenture.com/us-en/insights/strategy/trust-in-business?c=strat_competitiveagilmediarelations_10394050&n=mrl_1018.

18 Kiel, F. (2015). *Return on character: The real reason leaders and their companies win*. Boston, MA: Harvard Business Review Press.

19 Kiel, F. (2015). Leadership measuring the return on character. *Harvard Business Review, 93*(4), 20–21.

20 Industry Week. (February 26, 2019). Being ethical has its perks: World's most ethical companies. *Industry Week*. Downloaded from: https://www.industryweek.com/leadership/companies-executives/article/22027217/being-ethical-has-its-perks-worlds-most-ethical-companies.

21 Ibid.

9 Your challenge

When you're baking a cake, if certain ingredients aren't included or the instructions aren't followed, things probably won't turn out as planned.

Similarly, in organizational settings, if you cut corners when it comes to ethics, you can end up with a recipe for corruption.[1] Here are the ingredients:

1. The organization's strategy and/or performance metrics justify engaging in questionable acts.

DOI: 10.4324/9780429324284-10

2. Small steps are taken toward engaging in unethical behaviors, which gradually increase in magnitude and frequency.
3. Those in authority *appear* to be just.
4. Leaders who *seem* understanding suddenly become dictatorial.
5. Rules are vague and changing.
6. Actions that legitimize questionable or unethical performance are rewarded.
7. You and those you work with are expected to comply.
8. It is difficult to quit (exit).[2]

Research by Philip Zimbardo, Professor Emeritus at Stanford University (known for his Stanford prison experiment), contributes to our understanding of what factors lead to a breakdown in morality. His controversial 1971 study asked undergraduate volunteers to role-play prison guards and prisoners set up to engage in a mock prison in the basement of the university's psychology building. Within 24 hours, things began to get out of hand, as the acting guards used brute force on some of the inmates. The experiment was cut short, given the inappropriate behaviors demonstrated by those participating. Zimbardo's findings are in keeping with Milgram's classic research (as previously described). The list outlined above was derived from Zimbardo's ongoing pursuit of how to better understand how and why good people might choose to engage in acts of immoral behavior.

We sometimes refer to moral decay in organizational settings as "sliding down a slippery slope." Any one of those ingredients described (above) can contribute to an ethically volatile situation. When combined, they become a crucible in which unethical behavior can form, grow, and thrive. We must learn to pay attention, preventing such circumstances from happening around us and catching us off guard.

To ensure that this doesn't happen to you, let's return to the idea of what you care about. Recall what you truly and deeply value. Complementing those values, as a businessperson, you want to do well. That means achieving success and making money.

You are what you measure

Unless performance metrics are structured in ways that account for how your goals are to be achieved, the race to make money and the drive to accumulate power can inadvertently create blind spots. Given our motivation to do well in business, we may set ourselves up for a clash in values.

Sometimes, it might seem like everything we care about is trying to get our attention. When we're at work, it can be hard to know what's right, especially when any of those ingredients for corruption are present.

People naturally tend to move in the direction of how their success is measured. If your company consistently emphasizes the need to nail a target, hit a number, and/or make a deadline, it's easy to forget about the means of achieving your goals. It's likely that you

and your co-workers will focus predominately on the outcomes, i.e., the bottom line.

There's truth to the adage, "You are what you measure."

Our Western consumer-oriented economy is framed this way. So even if the company you work for effectively rewards ethical performance, the quarterly reporting system, in largess, may actually work against business ethics.

Hard target demands generally reinforce short-termism.

My Company is committed to climate change... causing it, that is!

Some companies might also say they are concerned about global warming, human rights, poverty, and a host of other social issues. Corporate social responsibility (CSR) is of vital importance. But our livelihoods, retirement accounts, and education are often inextricably bound up in the immediacy of return on investment (ROI).

One way or another, we are all affected by the embedded moral hypocrisy of the culture around us.

We see this day in and day out.

When someone says they're "doing good" it almost always has less to do with morality and more to do with profit margins. In the twenty-first century, *goodness* has become largely synonymous with commercial achievement. Unfettered capitalism largely means establishing unseemly profits for unbounded selfish interests.

Wouldn't it be nice if "doing good" was actually about doing good?

Here's a question we all need to ask ourselves:

Do we want to build morality into business?

If the answer is yes, how would we go about this effort?

To begin to address this question, we have to start with ourselves. Each person needs to value their own moral identity. It's important to recognize how easy it is to get tripped up, not only by the situation or context, but by one's own primitive instincts and basic natural tendencies. We must learn to actively look for the ethical issues that are a part of our work, rather than waiting for ethical problems to emerge. Once these issues are identified, we can practice responding to them with moral courage and other character strengths.

Into action

Rather than waiting for problems to hit the fan and then reacting to them, we can seek out moral engagement. From there, we can rehearse effective thought-action practices. This is what we call a proactive approach to ethical behavior.

Let's make this effort real.

You can start to exercise your ethics by reflecting on an encounter you've already experienced.

Think of a time when you faced an ethical challenge at work.

In this situation, it may have appeared as though none of your options seemed favorable. The circumstances may have presented a conflict between your personal and professional values. It was likely that some level of tension or paradox was present when you worked to determine your action. It may have seemed as though your options would impose undesirable consequences. There may have been a strain between doing what you thought you should do and what social or organizational norms suggested. Perhaps there was a discrepancy between your personal ideology and your organization's goals. In short, it was difficult to act, to know what to do, or to know how to best resolve this situation. As you think back, this was a situation where you had a hard time determining what to do. It was likely a difficult circumstance because of the perceived risks that accompanied your taking action.

a) What was the context? Was there management pressure? Were you under a tight deadline?

_____

_____

b) At the time, what were you thinking?

_____

_____

c) At the time, what were you feeling?

_____

_____

d) What was the ethical issue?

_____

_____

e) What happened? What decisions were made?

_____

_____

f) What did you do?

_____

_____

g) Did you feel that the organization supported your ability to proceed with moral action?

_____

_____

Now that you have identified a personal example, think about what helped or interrupted your desire to proceed with an ethical response.

h) What activities, processes, behaviors in your organization supported your ability to proceed with a moral response?

_____

_____

i) What activities, processes, behaviors in your organization prohibited your ability to proceed with a moral response?

_____

_____

j) How do you feel about this event now, in retrospect?

_____

_____

Looking back on this experience, you can begin to see how you might react to circumstances when there's an ethical issue and when your moral identity is challenged.

Learning to see how, when, and where your character strengths show up and are put into action (or when you hold back from exercising them) is important. That is, if you want to improve your ability to respond to ethical issues at work.

Have you ever benched a value, virtue,
or character strength because hitting a
performance goal seemed more important?

Building your moral muscle is not about success or failure. It's about understanding what circumstances might prohibit you from having a desire to be your best self.

If you want to improve, getting to know yourself is key.

Here are some questions you can ask yourself to increase your self-awareness:

Are you worried about what others will think of you?

Are you concerned about letting your boss or team member down?

Are you afraid of not getting your bonus?

Are you nervous about calling attention to yourself?

Are you afraid about how your actions (or inactions) might affect your career?

Are you apathetic?

As you reflect upon your workplace challenges, continue to think about what you can do today to strengthen your capacity to look for and respond to the ethical issues that challenge you.

Outline three specific steps that you can take, ideas that you can apply, which will help you defend, protect, and demonstrate your moral identity in the workplace:

1. _____

2. _____

3. _____

   _____

Strength #9: Learn from your past to build a more ethical future.

Notes

1 Zimbardo, P. G. (2007). *The Lucifer effect: Understanding how good people turn evil.* New York: Random House.
2 Zimbardo, P. G. (2004). A situationist perspective on the psychology of evil: Understanding how good people are transformed into perpetrators. In A. Miller (Ed.) *The social psychology of good and evil* (pp. 21–25). New York: Guilford Press.

10 Your workout routine

Just as we attend to our physical health, we must take responsibility for our ethical well-being. We must exercise our ethicality if we want our moral identity to be there when we need it. To get ourselves ready, we have to build up the skills that support an ability to demonstrate moral courage.

If you were able to come up with three steps to defend, protect, and exercise your moral identity at the end of the last chapter, congratulations! You may be ahead of the game. If you were stumped or uncertain, don't worry. Just read on. Everyone can learn how to improve by establishing an ethics workout routine. As a start to this effort, some steps you can implement right now, today, include the following:

- Showing an extra courtesy, kindness, or lending a helping hand to a co-worker, customer, or stranger
- Bringing some much-needed patience and empathy to a tense or difficult moment

DOI: 10.4324/9780429324284-11

- Holding your tongue if what you are thinking of saying isn't thoughtful or necessary
- Requiring those you do business with to address their stakeholder issues
- Spending some extra time to garner information, recheck calculations, proofread your work, run your ideas by others, taking a few extra precautions to ensure accuracy, and/or improve the quality of your efforts
- Identifying an ethical issue and coming forward, presenting the situation with honest and forthright clarity.

When attempting to accomplish anything, whether it's running a marathon, writing a book, or baking a cake, you have to practice. Very few recipes come out perfectly on the very first try! In some cases, this means making certain activities a part of your everyday routine.

If you want to get better at something, you need to do it over and over again, continuing to work at it, improve, and then striving to make it your best. Over time, practice becomes a skill, which can eventually become second nature to you.

For example, to get into physical shape, you would not start jogging five miles on day one. You might begin by walking, picking up the pace, and gradually increasing your distance. Then, over time, you build up your stamina and capacity for endurance.

We cannot expect people in the workplace to be effective at dealing with ethical decision-making after a two-hour online training course. While important, ethics training typically provides rule-based content and then quizzes you on that information. Sure, you might tick the box on having fulfilled the legal demand for compliance training. But does this type of activity develop your moral competency?

Training alone is not enough to build moral strength in the workplace.

Let's get real

Some people don't even take employee training seriously. For example, I heard a bunch of people yelling letters down the hallway one day. I thought to myself, "What the heck are they talking about?" So, I went up to one of the guys and said, "What do the letters stand for?" He said, "Oh, those are the answers to the organizational ethics quiz we have to take."

Right.

OK then.

That's not very encouraging.

*Cheating on the organizational training quiz
does not bode well for ethical development, now
does it?*

A best-case scenario is that this approach can
potentially increase employees' awareness of the importance of this information. That's a good starting
point. Rules-based knowledge is vital to organizational
ethics. But how does this information help to build
the requisite skills needed to actually engage in moral

action? Can knowing the rules translate into supporting your ability to demonstrate moral strength? What
about the ability to build your desire to respond to an
ethical challenge when you're at work?

Hmmm, probably not.

If we're lucky, the results of these kinds of program-
matic efforts help to ensure that employees are mindful of the laws, rules, and corporate policies. Awareness
of "the rules" suggests that people will then choose to
abide by them.

I wish we could count on that being 100% true.

But it's not.

As such, we need to return to honing and exercising
our character strengths. This is also known as adopting a virtue-based approach. It may seem obvious, but
we all need to be reminded to treat others the way we
want to be treated. Today's *Platinum Rule* goes a step
beyond the *Golden Rule* (suggesting that we should
treat others the way they expect to be treated).

Plato would suggest that your happiness and well-
being are paramount. A way to secure *eudaimonia*

(Greek), which means to flourish by living a life well, is by executing your virtues.[1] This will, however, require some self-discipline. Well, that is if you hope to attain either of the above life goals. As a proponent of justice, Plato would likely agree that rules are important to help foster ethical behavior.

The problem is that rules can do little or nothing to prepare employees for how to deal with and manage the emotionally charged elements of an ethical situation. Learning to identify and face an ethical challenge, and then working through how to best tackle the particular concern, require special skill sets (also known as moral competencies). When we see the ethical elements embedded within the decisions we make, we create pathways for our virtues to shine. Virtues can also be referred to as one's character strengths.

Dealing with an ethical issue must be managed as you navigate your competing values, which presumably include being empathetically present for other's needs.

While you may want to be ethical, you may also want to hit your performance goals, be liked by your peers, not draw attention to yourself, and not cause problems for your boss.

Whoa, this is starting to sound like work.

No worries! Once you get the hang of it, the effort can be second nature to you.

Why not offer employees a more robust approach to ethics than just focusing on the rules? Let's build the capacity for moral strength using an exercise routine that applies to their everyday work life. By practicing specific skills that we know support moral action, and exercising them a tad each day, people can gradually get more comfortable with their application and use. This method helps employees prepare for effective ethical engagement.

Rather than rote learning via memorization, a more meaningful method to teaching business ethics is one that's associated with people's own lived experiences. What's more, it includes active participation in an on-going manner.

You already began the activity when you responded to the prompts in the last chapter. You paused and reflected on your own ethical encounters and unpacked the situation to better understand your thoughts, feelings, and motivations for acting or not acting in an ethical manner.

Most companies teach ethics based on the idea that if everybody knows what's illegal and is aware of corporate policy, the organizational ethics are "good to go." Employees pass the multiple-choice quiz and they're all set until the next email comes around, saying it's time for the annual requirement to be fulfilled again. The general premise is that knowing the rules prevents rule breaking.

Fine. OK.

That works.

Until it doesn't.

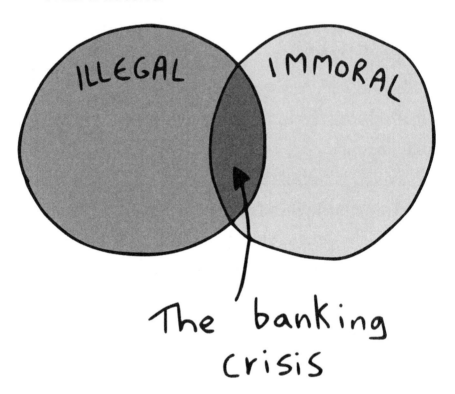

The banking crisis

Recognizing that people are notorious rule-benders (especially in business, where situations often encourage and normalize this kind of behavior), organizational scholars realized we must do more.[2] Additional work in this area led to beefed-up training, now guiding employees recognize ethical issues.

The idea was to help people become more aware of the challenges they might face in their particular area.[3]

Fine. OK.

That works.

Until it doesn't.

While this "value-add" is certainly an advancement, the problem is that much of the time, people don't think before they act. Point being, we aren't as rational as we believe ourselves to be. We sometimes, without even realizing it, proceed with an action and then apply a rationale for whatever we did, *after* we do it.

You might get better at identifying issues. But when you're in the middle of a stressful workday (with hundreds of priorities demanding your attention), are you really going to stop and think about the variables that might impact the short- and long-term implications of your response-actions in that moment?

Probably not.

Using a decision-making model can be helpful. But its practical real-time application may be unlikely. This

is especially the case if you're in the middle of a pressing and stressful ethical issue.

While management's motives may have been good, when the U.S. Navy issued moral decision-making wallet cards for every junior officer, I thought, "Is this really going to help increase ethical action?"

Can you envision officers whipping out their ethics card when they have to deal with decisions?

Some suggested an ethical decision-making app would be a great idea. Alas, we run into the same problem. It's "fun" to play around with. But does it actually help increase prudent decision-making when dealing with ethical issues at work?

With each person, situation, and context being unique, apps are largely overly simplistic, and thus not particularly useful for real-time functionality. To help employees dealing with situational stressors of an ethical response decision, we have to do more.

Certainly, an awareness of how to make effective decisions is key. But this approach, unto itself, is woefully incomplete for dealing with ethical concerns. We need to help people learn how to employ personal governance, enabling application of their values, virtues, and character into the decisions they make.

A particular challenge is that human beings tend to act and then explain why they selected a particular response after they engaged. We can become great at post-hoc justification, not cognitive decisions that are purposeful and deliberate. Given our propensity to tell ourselves stories about why we do things AFTER we do them, we have to engage learners to see the ethical elements within every decision.

More specifically, it's important to employ specific skills that underwrite your moral strength.

What Mr Rogers, Peppa Pig (snort), Lisa, Arthur, Dora, and Daniel Tiger already know

They deliberately think about how to do what's right.

The secret is found in taking a moral development approach to ethics. This is learning how to practice the

L.E.D.
LIGHT BULB
(BEST FOR ETHICAL IDEAS)

skills that will help you build moral competency. It's a path that helps you regularly apply your virtues with deliberate intent.

This method will help you reduce the potential for ethical issues emerging on your doorstep. When they do happen (and they will), you can be ready! You will have developed your capacity to face them with moral courage.

Once you practice identifying the ethical elements within each of your decisions, you can continue to enhance your capacity for moral strength. Your ability to effectively respond to an ethical challenge can be bolstered by learning four recommended skills. The moral competencies are the following:

1. Emotional signaling
2. Reflective pause
3. Self-regulation
4. Moral reinforcement

So now let's take a look at what they mean and how they work.

#1 Emotional signaling

Emotions are important tools. They fuel our thoughts, providing important clues for where we should direct our attention. This innate mechanism gives us the ability to derive options, ways to react to any given situation.

Emotions offer up important signals that play a critical role in motivating movement or hindering progression to engage in a moral response-action. We need to learn how to read these signals correctly and not just blindly react to them.

If you don't manage your emotions, they will manage you.

Emotions can be interpreted differently. But suppressing or ignoring them doesn't make their impact go away. It just means the feelings will express themselves in less deliberately managed outlets (e.g., behavioral flare-ups, anxiety, and even depleting your immune system). Negative emotions signal a cause for concern, which can trigger the fight-or-flight response.

You know the feeling, it goes something like this:

HEY!

It's time to get out of here!

Duck and cover.

Or, get ready and put up your dukes!

These cues are survival-oriented. They are hardwired into our framework, so that we can endure (e.g., protecting ourselves and loved ones).

I don't doubt that some folks might find their daily activities in the workplace similar to survival on the Serengeti. For example, I've actually been told in an organizational setting, "You need to see someone higher up in the food chain," when seeking assistance.

And yet, the reality is that it is highly unlikely you will "eat or be eaten" in the workplace. Figuratively speaking, however, many organizations encourage this kind of talk to prompt competition and motivate goal achievement.

How do you think this kind of talk makes people feel about the value of their work and their contribution?

This language is not helpful if you're trying to support ethical performance in your organization!

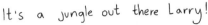

We see that some companies use their performance metrics to make it seem like the workplace is based upon the survival of the fittest.

> *The late Jack Welch was known for implementing this type of approach at GE in the 1980s.*

When people have to make targeted goals to win bonus pay, or when only a limited number of people can rise to the next level, it can begin to feel like a jungle. In short, it feels like you have to fight to stay alive.

This creates a potentially unhealthy organizational culture, one that may enable unethical behavior. When unbridled competition is present, it fuels a workplace where some will try to take credit for others' work, make up facts to suit their own purposes, and where greed can saturate business operations.

However, when negative emotions stir attention to morality, they can play an important role in maintaining the organization's ethical health. Certain sentiments are often piqued when employees encounter an ethical issue. Feelings like worry, loneliness, fear, shock, or surprise, and even anger or a sense of being harmed often accompany awareness of an ethical issue.

Facing a problem, striving to find the ethical element within a decision, and learning to recognize ethical risks in business come with affective (emotional feeling) experiences. Your body is telling you to pay attention and to take care.

Listen to your emotional signals.

It's interesting that awareness of an ethical issue may be associated with hurt feelings. This often stems from a sense of betrayal. We see this occur when a person perceives that someone (e.g., a co-worker, colleague, peer, or someone in power) has behaved unethically. Either that, or this person is doing nothing to address

'Emotional Suppression'
25 YARDS !

an ethical concern that they said they cared about, and/or should have at least been aware of, and be making moves to address. The reality is that in some cases people who should respond to the issue will not.

Worse yet, they may be a part of the ethical issue itself.

Being aware of one's emotional cues and using them to foster movement toward moral action is called emotional signaling. Emotional signaling can be used to help navigate and manage how one reacts to unethical circumstances. Rather than ignoring the problem, lashing out, or becoming part of it, employees can learn to experience negative emotions as signals that they are aware and need to protect and defend their moral identity.

> *You cannot say you care about ethics in the workplace and turn away from an ethical issue.*

> *You have to step up and do something about it.*

Awareness that emotional feelings are drivers for impulsive actions then provide cues to be cautious, slow down, and consider that there's been a red flag thrown on the moment, activity, situation, project, and/or further engagement. This means closer review is warranted, before you do anything.

Now that you have started to listen to your internal affective cues you need to know what to do with the signals you are receiving. Identify three ethical issues that you have encountered in the workplace, on a team or group, or in a business transaction.

1. _____

2. _____

3. _____

_____

List some specific emotions that you felt when you discovered the issue, worked through it, and resolved or got beyond it:

1. _____

2. _____

3. _____

_____

Note: Feeling "good" or "bad" is incomplete. If you're unsure what descriptive terms are available, this link provides key terms and descriptors: https://www.healthline.com/health/list-of-emotions.

#2 Reflective pause

A reflective pause is a self-imposed moment to stop and consider if it is in your best interest, or in the best interest of others, to act. The imposition of a "time-out" before doing anything actually supports ethical behavior in the workplace. In pausing, there is time to weigh the pros and cons of acting (or not acting) in a particular way, considering past and/or potential behaviors, as well as their possible implications.

People who learn to self-impose a reflective pause can harness their emotions and other situational factors to support response-actions that are morally grounded.

Taking a moment to center oneself is important.

Breathe.

Reflection slows down the impulsivity that compulsions or thoughtless responses might invoke.

When ethical issues emerge and emotions are roused, employees can learn to take a step back for a moment. People known to engage in morally courageous responses to ethical challenges recognize the value of pausing before doing anything.

When did you last make a concerted effort to deliberately pause?

Practice imposing a short time-out. Take a moment to collect your thoughts before you make your next decision. In that time, consider the ethical elements of your choice and response-action.

Now, try this a few times throughout your day.

Recognize that negative emotions may be a sign that your moral identity is being called to duty. While your initial reaction may be to turn away, ignore, or avoid addressing the cause of a negative reaction, during this pause you can learn to see that your emotions (albeit unpleasant) are signaling you to respond to the ethical issues at hand.

Once you identify an ethical issue and become aware of your emotions, instead of reacting, take some time to pause and reflect on the situation. Practicing this skill, describe: a) what you did during this self-imposed break, b) if the time-out was beneficial to you, and c) why (or why not).

a) _____

b) _____

c) _____

#3 Self-regulation

Parents have discovered the value of self-control, especially when their two-year-olds display the lack of it. Self-regulation turns out to be an essential element of moral action, and, thus, it is at the heart of human welfare. And yet, this skill remains a vastly underrated virtue throughout most of society. The capability to resist acting on our impulses, especially when facing challenging circumstances, is crucial to our ability to be ethical in business. Unfortunately, Western culture promotes and encourages instant gratification, thereby reducing the value of self-regulation in society overall.

Self-regulation represents a conscious choice to control our first reactions, those impulses that circumstances might generate. While it takes effort, you can choose to modulate your behavior in accordance with your values, beliefs, and the goals that you are striving to achieve.

Your first thoughts do NOT have to be the ones you ultimately apply. I can think of many occasions where my first thoughts were decidedly NOT the right thing to do (quit, throw something, yell/scream, etc.). In addition, when you purposively impose self-regulation you can override temptations that prompt your inner voice to say, "just ignore it," "going with the flow is easier," "everyone else is doing it," "it's not my problem," "I don't want to be the snitch," and so forth. Instead, you recognize that saying and/or doing nothing is **not** in keeping with your values, beliefs, and personal code of honor.

Once you start identifying ethical issues, you can practice modifying your internal scripts. Instead of saying to yourself, "it's not my job," you recognize your role, and tell yourself, "it's important that we do something about this," "nothing changes unless I stand up and help create change," "this issue came my way for a reason and it's on

my watch," "we need to address this or it will just continue," and/or "I must live the values I say I hold."

Hello personal accountability!

My friend and colleague at the University of Michigan, psychologist Rick Bagozzi, explains how one's internal scripts can help you manage your moral identity. You can ask yourself questions like:

Is this what my Granddad (Mom, Dad, wife, partner, children) would expect of me?

Is acting (or not acting) in keeping with the beliefs I say I hold?

Is acting (or not acting) worthy of pride?

Is acting (or not acting) worthy of shame, guilt, or embarrassment?

Are my actions in keeping with the way I was raised?

If everyone acted this way, would it make for a better (or worse) world?

Self-regulatory processes usher motivational resources that can help you choose to give up short-term gains to attain future goals. If you're tempted to do or say nothing when an unethical situation arises, you can learn to draw upon your moral emotions (shame, guilt, pride), thinking about how you would feel if your response to the situation became known.[4]

Eventually, everything comes out in the wash.

There are no secrets.

As a honed skill, self-regulation can be used to direct your energy toward the affirmation of your moral identity. It is a choice to impose self-control, and then to proceed by engaging in moral action.

Think of three examples where you imposed self-regulation and how it proved to be useful (while working with others, at home, shopping, etc.).

1. _____

2. _____

3. _____

_____

#4 *Moral reinforcement*

Learning from your past actions is a practice, one that can be honed and fine-tuned. It's the ability to draw insight from your prior experiences, servicing as fodder for your own moral development.

This practice can help increase your capacity to effectively attend to the next ethical challenge that comes your way. After this incident has been attended to, it's important to gather your thoughts during post hoc reflection, once you have responded to the concern, faced it, decided what to do, and then acted. Moral reinforcement calls attention to where you have done well, recognizing the virtues that are part of your core. It also petitions you to examine where your weaknesses reside. From that point, you can build your moral muscle strength, better understanding where you need to exercise and improve.

Self-analysis and critique can prepare you for the next challenge, thinking in advance of how you might respond, perhaps more effectively, in the future. It's also a way to consider how to prevent ethical issues from happening over and over again. Importantly, it can also give you a better understanding of what

And pause, and reflect, and learn! Let's get ethical!

circumstances to avoid and how to prevent ethical lapses from occurring in the first place.

Learning from your mistakes and preparing for the future can help support a sustained awareness of your moral identity. And, like all the other moral competencies, it can be practiced and applied in the workplace.

> *Knowing isn't enough to change behavior; we have to put knowledge into action.*

Taking the time to recognize and evaluate your behaviors, coupled with discerning how to improve upon them, makes your moral competency workout one that can continue to be enhanced over time. Exercising your moral identity will build your character strength, providing you with a more consistent and reliable best self.

As you reflect on the ethical issues you have faced, what did you learn from these experiences? What specific key nuggets of wisdom did you garner as a result of your actions (or lack thereof)? What helps you move toward moral engagement? What tends to mitigate your desire to act?

1. _____

2. _____

3. _____

_____

Taking inventory can raise points that can be used to bolster your ability to engage in ethical action in the future. See where your strengths are leveraged and where you can do better. Importantly, business ethics is not something that is fixed, rigid, or a topic you can memorize. It is the application of your moral identity in the workplace, woven into the fabric of your organizational life.

If you are reminded and troubled by ethical acts of the past, behaviors that you or others engaged in, you can reclaim your moral identity, rebuild your

strengths, and create a more responsible future. We can all learn from both good and bad examples. The idea is to role-model the behaviors you want to see around you.

> *The world tends to reflect back to us what we project.*

To ensure your ethical health and that of the company you work for, you can build up your moral competency, specific skills that support the ability to proceed with a moral response when faced with an ethical issue. As you identify the ethical components within every decision you make, be sure to exercise your moral muscles. Emotional signaling, reflective pause, self-regulation, and moral reinforcement are the moral competencies that will fortify your every move.

Strength #10: To protect your moral identity, give it a workout!

Notes

1 Frede, D. (2017). Plato's ethics: An overview. *The Stanford Encyclopedia of Philosophy* (Winter 2017 ed.), Edward N. Zalta (ed.). Downloaded from: https://plato.stanford.edu/entries/plato-ethics/.
2 Sekerka, L. E., & Zolin, R. (2007). Rule bending: Can prudential judgment affect rule compliance and values in the workplace? *Public Integrity, 9*(3), 225–244.
3 Sekerka, L. E. (2009). Organizational ethics education and training: A review of best practices and their application. *International Journal of Training and Development, 13*(2), 77–95.
4 Ajzen, I. (1991). The theory of planned behavior. *Organizational Behavior and Human Decision Processes, 50,* 179–211.

11 Get a posse

Celebrated cases of whistleblowing are certainly heralded acts of individual moral courage. But solo reporting is not a requirement for moral excellence.

Being ethical in the workplace does not mean you have to go it alone.

DOI: 10.4324/9780429324284-12

If you observe an ethical concern, an important step is to report it. A tool many large organizations offer is the anonymous hotline. In the U.S., the Sarbanes-Oxely Act of 2002 (as a result of the Enron Scandal) mandated corporate reporting channels. Publicly traded firms are required by law to provide whistle-blower hotlines and organizational ethics training.[1]

Employees are encouraged to ring this hotline number if they observe an unethical activity. But it doesn't have to be a *bona fide* ethical issue to justify a call. Many organizations encourage their members to use reporting tools if they think an ethical impropriety might be occurring, or if the company is at risk for an unethical event.

That is, before it occurs!

Creating a sense of openness for sharing ethical concerns is a central feature of organizational transparency. The provision of "safe spaces" is a recognizable feature of effective organizational ethics. I have already provided examples to illustrate how some firms have done the complete opposite. Another profound story was presented by Susan Fowler, who wrote about her year at Uber. She found the organization's culture to be one of gender discrimination, harassment, and bias.[2] After blowing the whistle with a blog of her experiential account, her case went public and she was named as one of *Time* magazine's People of the Year as a "silence breaker."[3]

Recognizing the value of reporting, some firms have taken proactive approaches. At Gap Inc., they encourage their employees to freely communicate with their global ethics department, either via the hotline or by contacting them directly. This company wants to prevent ethical issues from occurring by welcoming employee concerns.

Ethical challenges may emerge in the form of discrimination and harassment. Or they can manifest as an observation that something just doesn't seem "right."

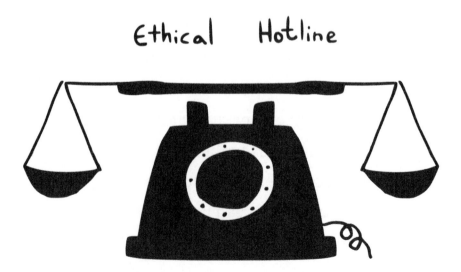

Ethical Hotline

They may be concerns related to the rights of an individual, or problems related to protecting the integrity of the company. Some issues are on a broad scale, impacting humanity and/or the natural environment.

Unethical extremes emerge when there is a lack of attention to basic human rights. A case in point is the situation when Apple and Hewlett-Packard subcontracted workers at a factory in China, known as FoxConn. Employees felt overworked, used, and controlled. Some responded by jumping from windows (to their deaths) to protest the working conditions. Rather than considering a change to the working conditions the company installed nets.[4] This response sparked media attention, fueling international outrage. Eventually the employees' wages were increased, but so was their quota. Their residential and controlled lifestyle within the factory remained unchanged. The oppressive situation was not altered, and the story disappeared once it left the headlines. Human rights violations are tremendous concerns, which we must all be aware of and address via sustained consumer, citizen, and organizational activism.

The issues you face and address with moral courage drive the future of ethics in business.

In the U.S., we have a right to a safe and healthy workplace. We must ensure that that right is protected by giving voice if these conditions are not present.

You can be a voice to promote and encourage what is right, good, and true.

You can be a voice of dissent!

Help prevent or stop activities that are wrong, unethical, harmful, and/or dishonest.

We all need to step up and address these concerns in a moral manner. If everyone does their fair share of the lifting to improve the ethicality in their own sphere of influence, each engagement can make a HUGE difference. Each act can increase systemic change.

We must all take part in being a positive influence toward ethical change.

Chip in!

Put your character strength into your work.

Look for the ethical issues in your organization and see how you can add morality to the environment you're a part of.

Is your ethical issue listed?

Working with a number of professionals who specialize in leading ethics within their company, studying organizational ethics for over a decade, and teaching thousands of business ethics students at the executive, graduate, and undergraduate levels, I've heard thousands (really) of questions, concerns, and issues over the years.

Here are a few classic examples, which will give you an idea of the broad scope and nature of these concerns. Do you recognize any of these issues? Perhaps your ethical issue is listed below:

My boss criticizes my wearing a hijab. It's who I am.

Is it OK to mention my own jewelry line to our customers in case they might be interested in buying from me directly?

My manager (team member, subordinate, peer, etc.) seems hung over almost every day. What should I do?

The supervisor suggested that I fudge some numbers. She calls it "rounding up," but I don't feel comfortable doing this.

The company needs to provide more flexible hours so that I can take care of my baby.

Can I date my co-worker (team member, boss, manager, subordinate, etc.)?

I saw someone take an office chair home. What should I do?

I'm not getting any work breaks. Is this legal?

I've been asked to shave my beard. Do I have to abide by this instruction?

Everyone gets better hours than me. I think there needs to be a more equitable process of scheduling.

The nails used in our product are subpar. They do not meet the minimum standards we claim to represent.

I don't like the color of my office; it gives me headaches.

I take issue with the way we're calculating our performance metrics, but no one else sees a problem with it.

A co-worker keeps asking me to cover for them. I didn't mind at first, but it's starting to feel weird.

People cheat on their timecards. I really don't want to report it, because it's convenient to do this if you need to leave early.

I'm sure they had sex in the broom closet. Do I report them both, or just one of them?

The selling tactics used here depend upon making false claims and luring people to buy things they don't fully understand.

People are cutting corners on the number of tests we are supposed to perform before releasing the package.

A guy at work is sending me disgusting texts and says they're just a joke. I'm not laughing.

People are being promoted who cut corners to make quota. I'm being passed over, but I'm ensuring things are done "right."

My boss keeps looking at my chest. It makes me uncomfortable and nervous.

I am aware of the fact that someone made false claims on their resume. They already have the job, so is it a big deal?

There are plenty of ethical issues to go around. They come in all shapes and sizes. Just like people, they vary. Add to these concerns a host of circumstances and many nuanced perspectives, changing laws, and shifting policies. In 2020, there have been a surge of challenges related to pandemic protocols (both their presence and absence). Treatment and pay for essential workers and work-life balance present ongoing and evolving moral concerns.

Given the company, person, and situation, any issue could be viewed or interpreted in similar or different ways.

There are certainly blatant reprehensible actions, like bribery, payoffs, kickbacks, and fraud. But subtle forms of unethicality continue to evolve, as technological innovations are introduced. The collection of vast amounts of data enables surreptitious unethical activities to fester. Consider Facebook's ethics scandal. People learned that their personal information had been accessed by Cambridge Analytica without their knowledge, but it had actually been sold to them and other outside parties.[5]

Excuse me?

Where's my cut, for the use of my data
Facebook?

If you're going to sell my information, shouldn't I see some of that money you're getting for it?

It's one thing to find out that everyone knows I bought a raincoat, drive a Miata, and voted as an Independent. But it's an entirely new ballgame when you start to think about how a despicable operative might use everything about me (and everyone else I know) to incite harm. It's not a stretch before that information includes my health-care, employment, and other personal records and uses it in a twisted way that is strategically harmful. Propaganda leverages what people value and uses this information to entice fear and anger.

We've seen this reach all-time highs in the
modern era, given the power of social media.

While there are serious moral issues with the collection and use of big data, the responsibility in the Cambridge Analytica scandal resided with Facebook.[6] Their justification for the conflagration pointed to their mission to secure the freedom to communicate and share information in a "public form." The company was quick to blame everyone but themselves for the ethical disaster they created. Given that Facebook never offered a plausible explanation and deflected responsibility for what occurred, it's undeniable that consumers need to be wary of what appears to be "free." The use of communication channels has a price. When you use platforms like Facebook, Google, or Twitter, you have the opportunity to freely share your thoughts and opinions. But you are often giving away your personal data without your full knowledge or approval.

As a conduit of information, companies that hold our data have a moral obligation to protect it.

But they do not.

All too often innovators adopt the mindset that it's OK to take bold and unprecedented risks with their startup initiatives. I'm all for creativity and providing exciting, even radical new ideas in business enterprise. Waiting to ask moral questions until after ethical problems emerge is a recipe for corruption. What's more, many companies tend to push the cost of risk-taking onto their stakeholders.

That's you and me.

If you and your friends care about how your social media personas are used to monitor and potentially manipulate you, it's important for you to manage the situation, not let providers manage you.

You say you're too busy to think about this?

That's fine.

But you are likely to have to pay, eventually.

Ignorance is not bliss.

You don't have to go it alone

A lack of transparency will catch up with you and the organization you work for. It's just a matter of time. Left unaddressed, unethical operations are a ticking bomb, waiting to go off. Once it explodes, an ethical scandal depletes the value of a firm's stock and creates a legacy of reputational harm. At some point, you and I are the ones who will pay for the lack of business ethics. The costs show up in higher prices, a weakened economy, less stable employment, and fewer benefits— to highlight but a few of them. The degradation of trust in society can deplete our ability to flourish.

You certainly don't want to have to carry an added burden, one that's thrust upon you by those who lack moral responsibility. Corporations are supposed to add value to our lives, not give us cause for worry, doubt, anxiety, and stress. We must therefore look to those organizations that genuinely care about the short- and long-term interests of their stakeholders.

Ron Culp, a former head of public relations at Sears and now teaching crisis management at DePaul University, suggests that the role of government as the arbiter of societal ethics has shifted over to Corporate America.[7] For firms that do not step up to this duty, or that simply leverage virtue signaling (lofty words without actions), stakeholders will take their business elsewhere. For example, as America and countries around the world respond to the Black Lives Matter movement, corporate responses will need to go beyond the provision of a black square on Blackout Tuesday. Corporate boards, shareholders, and stakeholders need to work together to infuse sustained goals that are specific, measurable, and fully implemented, that ensure racial equity and justice in the workplace.

A clue that helps to discern a firm's ethical authenticity is how work is accomplished day in and day out. This is referred to as the organization's culture. Does your company foster complacency or silence when it comes to talking about ethics? Such an environment can deter even those with a strong moral identity from staying true to their core values. Given their anonymity, hotlines can help encourage reporting. And yet, they cannot be the sole source of how a firm upholds its ethical character. For starters, it's vital that the organization has multiple reporting channels. Research suggests that many employees would rather report an ethical problem directly to their manager than pick up the phone and make an official complaint.[8]

That's certainly not the case, however, if your manager or supervisor is part of the problem! Or, perhaps worse yet, if the company you work for supports unethical tactics to achieve its performance goals. There are also cases when concerns raised by employees have gone unaddressed and reporting channels did not prove to do the job that they were meant to accomplish. It's therefore essential that we recognize the possibility that reporting may turn out to be a protracted effort, and yes, harder than expected.

Take a step back and reconsider how we view the act of reporting.

When you encounter an ethical issue or assist a co-worker who is experiencing an unethical situation, it is important to document the incident. If you are comfortable speaking with the person(s) involved directly, that might be an option. But you can always share the information with your supervisor, ethics officer, or Human Resource Department. We already addressed the fact that employees should be encouraged to bring concerns forward before they become full-blown unethical malfeasance. Perhaps it's time to frame reporting as not so much a solo act, but as a team sport.

You do not have to go it alone.

We talk about coalition building in community, civic, or industry-based activities. This refers to when a group of people share a common interest and agree to work together to achieve a common goal. Initially, you might think of a coalition in reference to a civic-oriented operation, such as volunteering at a hospital, taking part in a beach or park cleanup, or giving service in some way to a local charity. It might be a more extended effort within your community, such as working to create reforms for human rights, addressing issues of justice, poverty, homelessness, or wildlife protection. The coalition could be part of a global initiative to protect civilians in areas of armed conflict, to fight global warming, or to protect access to clean water.

Coalitions are defined by their organizers and the issue at hand. And guess what? We can form them in the workplace as well! Coalitions are loosely formed associations designed to achieve a specific goal. Once achieved, they can disband.

In keeping with this idea, if you have a serious ethical concern it is often prudent to gather like-minded individuals together. In essence, you're joining forces to present the ethical concern to higher-ups in an organized manner. If you are worried you won't be heard, don't want to go it alone, or just want support, you can form a *posse*. Similar to a coalition, the idea of a posse is to gather like-minded organizational members together to address, report, and/or deal with an ethical concern within their company or even the industry writ large.

Moral courage in the workplace is about exercising your values and character strengths when it's a difficult circumstance. Worth noting is that people with moral courage rarely feel like engaging in moral action, but they do it anyway. They care about doing what's right and preserving their moral identity. They believe in the ethicality behind the work they're doing. They are willing to break the silence to ensure the company's integrity is genuine.

This is a tall order.

So forming a posse can be a very useful approach.

What's a posse?

The word *posse* stems from a Latin root (*posse comitatus*), referring to a group that helps keep peace or ensures laws are upheld. Maybe you've seen a vintage black-and-white TV Western where cowboys ride on horseback in pursuit of an outlaw. In juxtaposition to that picture, today's use applies to a group of people who share a common interest. For example, a posse that gets together to start a company or a group of friends who gather to have a tailgate party. Posse, as it's used in business ethics, refers to two or more people who connect around a shared ethical concern, with a goal to try and address it.

With reference to reporting an ethical issue in the workplace, the idea of forming a posse means to encourage collaborative strength, merge multiple forms of evidence, and bring together varying perspectives that can help bolster your reporting effort. A team approach to ethical reporting means that the responsibility is shared. This method prevents a lone reporter from enduring a sense of isolation and having to bear the burden alone.

By working with others, you can concentrate a collective focus on a particular problem and create alliances among those who may not normally work together. Moreover, if the reporting platform is large, isolated retaliatory measures may not be effective or even executed.

Broaching the reporting process as a team, you can also keep the approach consistent, so the effort is more streamlined and has less chance of falling through the cracks and/or being ignored.

There is strength in numbers.

What's more, working with others can help empower you to proceed with achieving corrective action. If you're in the unfortunate circumstance where management does not appear to want to hear your concerns, working together with other employees can also provide a support system.

In some cases, you may face a situation or circumstance when you must make the decision to step up to the plate alone and report an unethical event. Flying solo may be your last resort. If you have no other path and have to walk out on a limb, know that others may join your cause, in time.

Keep looking for support as you proceed!

True blood

The case of Theranos, Inc., a Silicon Valley "unicorn" startup, claimed to revolutionize blood testing. The company said it could perform blood tests but in a way that would require less blood and at far less cost than any existing procedure. Who wouldn't want to invest?

They didn't have the technology to accomplish what they claimed to provide.

They had the idea.

Uh-oh, that's a problem when people call your bluff.

Employee and whistleblower Tyler Shultz became aware of the fact that the company had doctored its research and ignored failed quality-control checks.[9] He wrote to Elizabeth Holmes, the founder of the company, explaining his concerns. She fobbed the issue off to Theranos President Sunny Balwani, who belittled Shultz for his lack of understanding basic laboratory science.

Shultz's response: I quit.

Upon doing so, Holmes curiously sent a warning through a member of Shultz's family. He should stop and consider what he would lose if he launched a vendetta against her blood-testing startup.[10] Shultz was unwavering in his claims. The company was fraudulent, and he knew it. He was unwavering in his resolve and demonstrated moral courage. But his bold initiative to share the truth ended up costing him and his family on multiple levels.[11] He had the support of his parents, who helped raise the money (selling their home) for legal fees. Holmes lobbed a legal battle, claiming he had violated the terms of the firm's nondisclosure agreement.[12] Undoubtedly, there were parts of his journey where he must have felt alone, anxious, bewildered, and angry.

A turning point came in 2015. Medical researchers John Ioannidis and Eleftherios Diamandis, and reporter John Carreyrou of *The Wall Street Journal*, launched a project to investigate the validity of Theranos' technology. It's important to note that the story itself may have been picked up by the *WSJ* because it carried an element of "stranger than fiction," which added human interest appeal.

Tyler Shultz happens to be the grandson of George Shultz, a former government official who served in various high-level positions under three different Republican presidents. George Shultz played a key role in shaping foreign policy under the Reagan administration. He was also a major figure in the Theranos scandal. He served on the firm's board and continued to support Holmes, even in the face of mounting evidence of fraud. While initially blind to the unethical scheme, George Shultz eventually praised his grandson (Tyler) for not having shrunk from "what he saw as his responsibility to the truth and patient safety, even when he felt personally threatened and believed that I had placed allegiance to the company over allegiance to higher values and our family."[13]

Learning from the disaster

In sharing his experience and story with Forbes in 2017, Tyler Shultz said he fully understood that entrepreneurs have to sell their vision. But, he added, they need to know the difference between the vision and "seeing something that's just not there."[14]

Once touted as a breakthrough healthcare technology company, by 2018 Theranos had become infamous for its false claims and duping investors out of $700 million. Once valued at $10 billion, the firm eventually folded under the weight of its own unethicality. Among the many lessons learned from this case, it's important to realize that ethical reporting does not have to be a solo act.

Get help!

Other employees emerged to join Tyler as fellow whistleblowers. Erika Cheung also stepped up in the effort to reveal the truth, making clear to federal regulators that she found Holmes to be a liar whose scheme had put patients' lives at risk.[15] Tyler Shultz and Erika Cheung turned their pain, passion, and learning from the experience into positive change. They created an organization called Ethics in Entrepreneurship. This not-for-profit portal is a place where whistleblowers can get hope, support, and advice. It's specifically designed for those working in the tech industry to help identify bad actors before they dup stakeholders.

It's not easy being cheesy (or ethical)

Speaking truth to power, bringing forward an ethical issue, and/or reporting a breach of ethics to someone with the authority to address it does not have to be performed in isolation. Recall the old adage, "a problem shared is a problem halved."

Well, it's true.

Taking the time to discuss ethical matters at work with trusted colleagues helps reduce stress levels.[16] When you report, plan a strategy with others first, and be sure to include self-care as a featured element of that path.[17] Whistleblowing does not and should not have to be a feared action.

Ethical concerns, risks, and issues are not going anywhere, so long as people are in business.

Therefore, framing ethical reporting as a shared duty needs to be a business priority.

Polling has found that 47% of the employees in the U.S. say that they have personally observed conduct that violates laws or their organization's standards. One could extrapolate and infer from that statistic that roughly half of your co-workers probably know about whatever ethical problem you may have observed.

If you know about it, chances are someone else does too.

Employees observing misconduct say that two-thirds of the incidents they see are recurring problems.

These patterns of unethicality often relate to external stakeholders and employees. Those reporting unethical activities in the workplace continue to increase, now at an all-time high, up 23% in the last two decades.[18] It's fair to note that reporting channels have expanded and may be capturing more information.

But are we changing any of the behaviors?

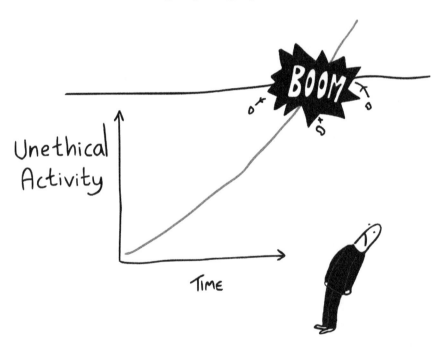

The Ethics & Compliance Initiative,[19] a group of nonprofit organizations that conducts organizational ethics studies, found that 16% of employees feel pressured to compromise their firm's own stated ethical guidelines.[20] One might extrapolate from this study, seeing how a person might take an annual ethics training class and then experience an organizational contradiction. What they're being asked to do to achieve performance is not in accordance with the ethical guidelines the company instructed them to adhere to.

The most frequently reported ethical issues in U.S. corporations are the misuse of confidential information, giving or accepting bribes or kickbacks, stealing, offering products or services that failed specifications, and sexual harassment.[21] Some industries seem to be particularly perilous for employees. For example, in a survey conducted by the Ethics & Compliance Institute, 39% of those in the accommodation and food services sector reported having observed at least one type of interpersonal misconduct, compared with 17% of employees in other professional services. In the U.K., the Institute of Business Ethics reports trends indicating that:

- Banking & Finance continues to be the sector with the most ethical lapses each year.
- The most common ethical issues relate to organizational behavior and culture, largely focusing on

sexual harassment, bullying, excessive professional pressure, misuse of social media, and cheating.

- Ethical issues pertaining to diversity and discrimination have increased by 50% (since their prior survey in 2018) and often relate to gender and pay inequities.[22]

Annual surveys and ongoing research suggest that there will always be pressure to cut ethical corners. When the culture encourages people to look the other way, enables questionable business practices to continue, and/or tolerates unethical activities, the behaviors are almost twice as likely to be accepted and even rewarded in the future.

The danger of organizational ethics hypocrisy cannot be overstated.

Ignoring the problems simply increases the likelihood that violations will appear over and over again. Moreover, they will increase in magnitude.

The solution?

Document everything.

Form a posse!

With each major case of ethical reporting we can see progress, if corrective action is taken and if learning occurs (i.e., change). However, sometimes it's a step backwards. If nothing is done to modify the cause of the issue, it will resurface again. This can be particularly distressing for those who speak out against unethical practices.

For example, in 2008, Anthony Menendez blew the whistle on energy giant Halliburton. He initially lost his job. He was then hired for his forensic expertise by GM.[23] As a forensic accounting litigation consultant he was honored by professional accounting associations for his endurance, resiliency, and commitment to stand by his charges. As far as Halliburton is concerned, the company treated him as though he were a traitor among the ranks as soon as he expressed concern about how they were booking revenue for warehouse goods. During his nine-year ordeal, he fought off the efforts of one of the world's biggest firms to silence him. Halliburton threw everything they could at him, orchestrating costly legal maneuverings. But with each blow, he bounced back. Even after Halliburton appeared to have won, Menendez, representing himself in the appeal, went to an Administrative Review Board, which overturned the original trial judge, by ruling that the company had engaged in whistleblower retaliation.[24]

Reflecting on his experience, he told me that, "Any incremental setback just increased my resolve."[25,26] Menendez proved to be a frontrunner in ethical reporting, helping to fortify whistleblower protection laws and to role-model moral courage in the workplace.

In 2014, with whistleblower protection and reward laws now in place, another whistleblower, this time at Monsanto, was awarded $22 million for fingering the agribusiness and chemicals conglomerate in another massive accounting fraud. The anonymous moral hero declared that society must do more. We need public demand to shape laws that will go after the leaders who enable this kind of corporate malfeasance.

In an interview with *The Washington Post,* he described how management is not held accountable for their unethical behavior. He explained that until this is corrected, these issues will continue to occur. With friction emerging in multiple areas of his life as a result of this case, his actions show how moral courage requires character strength from within and a personal commitment to right action. He explained, it's "something from deep within that drives you."[27]

Then, in June of 2020, Monsanto announced a settlement in its Roundup weed killer product litigation for over $10 billion. Bayer, the German-based company that acquired the agrochemical giant in 2018, said settlements in the U.S. would bring about 75% of claims to a close. The move came after years of claims, from over 95,000 cancer patients, that Roundup caused non-Hodgkin lymphoma and that Monsanto failed to adequately warn consumers of the product's risk. Bayer said the settlement agreements "contain no admission of liability or wrongdoing."[28]

> Examining Bayer's website, they state that: We exist to help people thrive Advancing health and nutrition is what we do best and care about most. Then they add: Our goal is to create value for our customers, stockholders, and employees, while also strengthening the company's earning power.[29] I don't know about you, but I detect an embedded conflict between care and money, with money coming in first place.

Shifting gears to another organization, Google employees have always been encouraged by the firm's leadership team to "act like owners." The firm's culture is one where "Googlers" engage in all sorts of forums, with specialized mailing lists, a meme generator, and open-ended question-and-answer sessions with top executives (known as T.G.I.F).

This is part of what it meant to be "Googley," which is one of the organization's value claims. Google's work ethic centers on free speech, openness, and positive deviance.[30] But when this internal activism began to defy corporate leaders' strategy for gaining profits, the company seemed confused by its own organizational identity.

Googlers followed their ideals, banding together to pool member resources, forming "posses" (small groups) for political activism. With social media becoming the new town hall or public square for society, some Google employees were concerned that, much like Facebook, they were becoming a disguised mechanism for advertising (or far worse). Engineers raised deep concerns that foreign governments were now exploiting the technology they created to influence domestic politics.

In 2017, activists within the firm shared their worries that Google had been co-opted for greater nefarious purposes (e.g., AI projects with the Pentagon/military). A growing number of workers believed initiatives like *Maven* were not in keeping with their values and wanted management to address this concern. Another project, *Anthos*, enables customers to combine their existing cloud services with Google. Google apparently provided the U.S. Customs and Border Patrol a trial of this product. This act outraged some of the company's engineers, who had been told that it was only intended for business use. Many employees began to leverage their access to Google mailing lists to express their moral outrage.

Employees weren't just organizing for external concerns. Groups were also organizing to protect themselves from discrimination and marginalization within Google's own organizational structure. In 2018, a highly coordinated 20,000-employee walk-out occurred, which generated global attention. And it wasn't just well-paid engineers and product leads who took part in this activity. Clerical and maintenance workers were also present, along with contractors and temps, determined to challenge their second-class status.[31] A handful of employees were then fired. Google explained how they "dismissed four individuals who were engaged in intentional and often repeated violations of our longstanding data-security policies." A spokeswoman from Google explained that "No one has been dismissed for raising concerns or debating the company's activities."[32] The results of the employee actions were mixed. Some organizational members reported feeling that the so-called shared ideals of Google and its employees to "do well and do good" had been betrayed. Others explained that the company had implemented strategies to achieve its combined share- and stakeholder goals.

As a former senior executive ethics leader at Google describes it, "Ethics is messy!" Andy Hinton, now a Silicon Valley ethics consultant and global ethics expert says, "It's not like you can gather all the information and then just get the right answer to resolve the ethical issue. When you have a lot of smart people in the room, you get a lot of great ideas. So you can have a lot of 'right' solutions on how to go about doing things. Figuring out how to sort through which path to choose is complex and time consuming; sometimes you have to change course. It's not easy."

Andy's contributions to business ethics education help young leaders better understand and appreciate how to deal in the "gray" areas of decision-making, while building a strong moral core. Andy knows that no matter how smart you are, human nature can kick in and thwart the best in all of us. He adds, with tongue and cheek, "Don't bet against stupid!" Referring to our blind spots, Andy is wise to the fact that people can be easily derailed by hubris, greed, and haste. Being humble is something Andy demonstrates and underscores as an essential ingredient in building organizational ethical strength.

At Facebook, a small but growing number of employees voiced concerns about the company's lacka-
daisical efforts to address false and misleading news.
Given the near-frenzied state of media hype, public
trust is influenced by the daily news feeds. People
typically seek out to confirm what they already believe to be true. Therefore, it's easy to see how our
beliefs can be manipulated. Facebook has been recal-
citrant in adopting rules and policies contributing to a
platform that enables people to lie. Those with money
and power can use social media for their own political
agendas and promote divisive propaganda. The firm
has had to deal with advertiser boycotts, which has
pushed down its stock price. As stakeholders demand
stricter policies to guard against hate speech, we will
see more (not less) of this sort of explicit engagement.
In June of 2020, Starbucks paused all of their social
media advertising with Facebook. Internally, Facebook continues to face a crisis of corporate morale,
with more than 5,000 employees denouncing the
company's decision to let a controversial comment by
the President of the U.S. remain posted.[33]

Both Google and Facebook are for-profit corporate
establishments. However, when capitalism drives a

wedge between shareholder and stakeholder interests, we can expect ethical challenges to emerge.

*The tension created when trying to increase the
value of a share and striving to uphold the values
at stake is the intersection of business and ethics.*

To discern this intersection, it must be discussed
openly. What we consider to be the ideal balance var-
ies, given who you are and where you stand. As such,
what is "right" is an emerging form, and one that may
not always have a set point determination. Thus, it
makes our struggle to pursue this quest for morality
in business all the more important.[34]

Perhaps just when we feel like giving up and throw-
ing in the towel on meaningful and sincere ethics in

corporations, we see moments when organizations suddenly rally into public service. Major corporations and countless other organizations offered gestures of goodwill during the Covid-19 pandemic of 2020–2021. Donations, matching funds, emergency response actions, loan programs, forgiveness policies, and a commitment to services prompted efforts to assist citizen stakeholders with support and information. Novel innovations were even created to help people understand, track, and learn more about health and safety.[35] When the pandemic hit, many firms vowed to help battle the crisis. Dozens of leading chief executives publicly pledged to focus less on shareholder returns and more on the well-being of their employees and broader communities. Some suspended investor payouts and vowed not to impose layoffs. But for a number of leading firms that was short-lived. As profits soared, companies sent tens of thousands of employees packing while billions went to shareholders. Walmart, Berkshire Hathaway, Disney, Salesforce, Cisco, Comcast, AT&T, Citigroup, Oracle, Microsoft, and other companies—presumed leaders in this charge—appeared to be back-pedaling from any long-term commitment.[36]

Like playing with clay, those who manipulate us are toying with the value of trust in our society. When this happens, uncertainty is fueled, which manifest in massive market swings.[37] In 2020, the Dow Jones and the S&P 500 suffered its worst percentage drop since 1987.[38] While the market has since made robust gains, it continues to be a mercurial casino-like venture. Given the majority of Americans no longer have pensions and must therefore deposit their savings in 401K investment-type strategies, their retirement monies are the gambling chips being used by industry moguls.

To create a more sustainable platform for business ethics, we can incorporate ethics within our performance goals—making them a required element of how we achieve corporate objectives. It is vital that we embrace moral action as a personal goal, in and of itself. While moments of crisis certainly require heroic response actions from organizations and individuals, everyday ethical behaviors fortify the backbone of society. Day-to-day virtuous acts indemnify your moral identity along with your organization's ethicality. Exercising your morality is an insurance policy that protects the values you say you hold by enacting them in your typical day-to-day interactions. But ethical response actions in the workplace may seem or feel like an effort in futility if the goal to perform your job ethically is not fully supported. This is especially difficult if you are experiencing an ethical issue and you cannot afford to take the risk of losing your job by giving voice to your values.

I mean, who CAN afford to lose their job?

Maybe it's that top 1%?

Giddyup!

As we traverse the roadways of life, in an organizational setting or otherwise, we must choose to be ethical. If you have decided you want to stand behind the value of your moral identity (both its worth and meaning), then you will be called to engage. Sometimes those who respond to an ethical issue with moral courage may have to endure personal risks and sacrifices. We are not all well-equipped to deal with unfavorable blowback that can include hostility, peer pressure, exclusion, legal actions, threats, or even being fired.

> *That's why you need to reach out and get moral support.*

The capacity to persist with morally courageous behavior, even when the initial act elicits rejection, resistance, or retaliation from within one's organization, is virtuous. The moral competencies you are now exercising daily will help prepare you for readiness and endurance.

Reporting, calling out ethical concerns, requires resilience that enables you and those you work with to forge ahead, even if backlash occurs. This capacity to persist adaptively in the face of adversity is not just useful for pursuing competition in the marketplace, it's central in defending and protecting your personal and organizational moral identity. Get your posse going, *before* you're in the middle of an ethical incident. You can get started by identifying three people at work that you would feel comfortable reaching out to if you see a questionable activity in your organization (first names only):

1. _____

2. _____

3. _____

_____

Now, reach out to them directly!

Yes, even though there may be no ethical issue at hand.

Or, you may have something in mind already.

Let them know that ethics in business is important to you. Discuss how you might work together to address an ethical issue or to correct an area of ethical risk that you currently see as troubling. It might be a situation that poses a threat to stakeholders if it continues as is. Given the advent of Covid-19 and the fact that many of us are now working from home (and may be doing so well into the future), it makes this outreach that much more important.

We all need to practice deliberate ethical communication before issues take hold. While texts and emails are fine for sharing information, make time right now to converse with the folks you've listed above. Talking with them explicitly about ethics in your organization is important. It's useful to discuss ethical concerns, risks, and issues that may be present now, or might develop, given your shared observations. Ask them about their insights and listen. After these conversations, describe several observations or key takeaways from them:

1. _____

2. _____

3. _____

  _____

Are they willing to support you in a time of need, were you to face an ethical issue at work?

Are you willing to support them?

Did they share your concerns?

Did you have ideas for how to engage corrective action?

People are out there who can and will support you. But you must continually seek them out. If you treat ethics in the workplace as an aspirational goal, you can ally with like-minded employees, those who also want to achieve similar aims.

Strength #11: Seek out help, until you have it.

Notes

1 Amadeo, K. (October 27, 2019). Sarbanes-Oxley summary: Four ways Sarbanes-Oxley stops corporate fraud. *The balance.* Downloaded from: https://www.thebalance.com/sarbanes-oxley-act-of-2002-3306254.

2 Fowler, S. (February 19, 2017). Reflecting on one very, very strange year at Uber. *Susan Fowler.com.* Downloaded from: https://www.susanjfowler. com/blog/2017/2/19/reflecting-on-one-very-strange-year-at-uber.

3 Zacharek, S., Dockterman, E., & Sweetland Edwards, H. (September 18, 2017). The silence breakers. *Person of the year 2017: TIME.* Downloaded from: https://time.com/time-person-of-the-year-2017-silence-breakers/.

4 Merchant, B. (June 18, 2017). Life and death in Apple's forbidden city. *The Guardian.* Downloaded from: https://www.theguardian. com/technology/2017/jun/18/foxconn-life-death-forbidden-city-longhua-suicide-apple-iphone-brian-merchant-one-device-extract.

5 Kelly, C. (April 8, 2018). Cambridge Analytica whistleblower: Data could have come from more than 87 million users, be stored in Russia. *CNN Politics.* Downloaded from: https://www.cnn.com/2018/04/08/ politics/cambridge-analytica-data-millions/index.html.

6 Leetaru, K. (March 19, 2018). The problem isn't Cambridge Analytica: It's Facebook. *Forbes.* Downloaded from: https://www.forbes.com/ sites/kalevleetaru/2018/03/19/the-problem-isnt-cambridge-analytica-its-facebook/#5fef9a0858a5.

7 Boyle, M. (June 5, 2020). Target's hometown tragedy unearths its struggles with diversity. *BNN Bloomberg.* Downloaded from: https://www. bnnbloomberg.ca/target-s-hometown-tragedy-unearths-its-struggles-with-diversity-1.1446474.

8 Muller, D. (September 11, 2018). Your company ethics hotline might not be enough. *HRAcuity.* Downloaded from: https://www.hracuity. com/blog/your-company-ethics-hotline-might-not-be-enough.

9 Carreyrou, J. (November 18, 2016). Theranos whistleblower shook the company—And his family. *The Wall Street Journal*. Downloaded from: https://www.wsj.com/articles/theranos-whistleblower-shook-the-companyand-his-family-1479335963.

10 Ibid.

11 O'Toole, J. (2008). Speaking truth to power. In W. Bennis, D. Goleman, and J. O'Toole (Eds.), *Transparency: How leaders create a culture of candor* (pp. 45–92). San Francisco, CA: Jossey-Bass.

12 Dunn, T., Thompson, V., Jarvis, R., & Louszko, A. (January 23, 2019). Ex-Theranos CEO Elizabeth Holmes says 'I don't know' 600-plus times in never-before-broadcast deposition tapes. *ABC News*. Downloaded from: https://abcnews.go.com/Business/theranos-ceo-elizabeth-holmes-600-times-broadcast-deposition/story?id=60576630.

13 Ibid.

14 Kincaid, E. (October 3, 2017). After blowing the whistle on Theranos, Tyler Shultz is going back into medical testing. *Forbes*. Downloaded from: https://www.forbes.com/sites/elliekincaid/2017/10/03/after-blowing-the-whistle-on-theranos-tyler-shultz-is-going-back-into-diagnostic-testing/2866029c575a.

15 Berke, R. (May 1, 2019). Stat, Business. From protégée to whistleblower: A former Theranos scientist says Elizabeth Holmes should 'come forward and apologize'. Downloaded from: https://www.statnews.com/2019/05/01/from-protegee-to-whistleblower-a-former-theranos-scientist-says-elizabeth-holmes-should-come-forward-and-apologize/.

16 Townsend, S. S., Kim, H. S., & Mesquita, B. (2014). Are you feeling what I'm feeling? Emotional similarity buffers stress. *Social Psychological and Personality Science, 5*(5), 526–533.

17 Comer, D., & Sekerka, L. E. (2018). Factors that contribute to durable moral courage in organizations. *Human Resource Management Review, 28*(2), 116–130.

18 Carucci, R. (December 16, 2016). Why ethical people make unethical choices. *Harvard Business Review*. Downloaded from: https://hbr.org/2016/12/why-ethical-people-make-unethical-choices.

19 Ethics & Compliance Initiative (ECI). (2018). Interpersonal misconduct in the workplace. *ECI/Ethics & Compliance Initiative*. Downloaded from: https://43wli92bfqd835mbif2ms9qz-wpengine.netdna-ssl.com/wp-content/uploads/2019/01/Global_Business_Ethics_Survey_2018_Q4_Final.pdf.

20 Ethics & Compliance Initiative (ECI). (2019). Workplace behaviors: A global outlook. *Global Business Ethics Survey: ECI/Ethics & Compliance Initiative.* Downloaded from: https://www.ethics.org/wp-content/uploads/2019-Global-Business-Ethics-Survey-4.pdf.

21 Verschoor, C. C. (July 1, 2018). Survey of workplace ethics. *SF: Strategic Finance.* Downloaded from: https://sfmagazine.com/post-entry/july-2018-survey-of-workplace-ethics/.

22 Institute of Business Ethics.org. (2019). Business ethics in the news 2019. *IBE: Institute of Business Ethics.* Downloaded from: https://www.ibe.org.uk/resource/business-ethics-in-the-news-2019.html.

23 Eisinger, J. (2015, April 21). The whistleblower's tale: How an accountant took on Halliburton. *ProPublica.* Downloaded from: http://www.propublica.org/article/the-whistleblowers-tale-how-an-accountant-took-on-halliburton (accessed 07/01/15).

24 Carozz, D. (May/June, 2016). He fought Halliburton and won: And interview with Tony Menendez, CFE, Sentinel Award recipient. *Fraud Magazine.* Downloaded from: https://www.fraud-magazine.com/article.aspx?id=4294992668.

25 Ibid.

26 Personal conversation with author, July 22, 2015.

27 Morgenson, G. (September 9, 2016). Monsanto whistle-blower: $22 million richer, but not satisfied. *The New York Times.* Downloaded from: https://www.nytimes.com/2016/09/11/business/for-monsanto-whistle-blower-a-22-million-award-that-fell-short.html.

28 Cohen, P. (June 24, 2020). Roundup maker to pay $10 billion to settle cancer suits. *The New York Times.* Downloaded from: https://www.nytimes.com/2020/06/24/business/roundup-settlement-lawsuits.html?campaign_id=60&emc=edit_na_20200624&instance_id=0&nl=breaking-news&ref=headline&regi_id=67225337&segment_id=31745&user_id=f217eaa47f4332408c7a00e3f7ee7090.

29 Bayer. (2020). Profile and organization. Downloaded from: https://www.bayer.com/en/profile-and-organization.aspx.

30 Cameron, K. S., & Spreitzer, G. M. (Eds.). (2011). *The Oxford handbook of positive organizational scholarship.* Oxford University Press.

31 Scheiber, N., & Conger, K. (February 18, 2020). The great Google Revolt. *The New York Times Magazine.* Downloaded from: https://www.nytimes.com/interactive/2020/02/18/magazine/google-revolt.html.

32 Ibid.

33 Dwoskin, E., Timberg, C., & Room, T. (June 28, 2020). Zuckerberg once wanted to sanction Trump. Then Facebook wrote

rules that accommodated him. Downloaded from: https://www. washingtonpost.com/technology/2020/06/28/facebook- zuckerberg-trump-hate/?location=alert&pwapi_token=eyJoeXAiOi JKV1QiLCJhbGciOiJIUzI1NiJ9.eyJjb29raWVuYW1lIjoid3BfY3JoaW QiLCJpc3MiOiJDYXJoYSIsImNvb2tpZXZhbHIioiNTk3YzExN WRhZGU0ZTI2NTE4ZDBkODAzIiwidGFnIjoid3BfbmV3c19hbG VydF9yZXZlcmUiLCJicmwiOiJodHRwczovL3d3dy53YXNoaW5nd G9ucG9zdC5jb20vdGGVjaG5vbG9neS8yMDIwLzA2LzI4L2ZhY2Vi b29rLXp1Y2tlcmJlcmctdHJ1bXAtaGF0ZS8_d3BtazoxJnd waXNyYz1hbF9uZXdzX19hbGGVydC1lY29ub215LS1hbGGVydC1w b2xpdGljcy0tYWxlcnQtbmF0aW9uYWwmdXRtX3NvdXJjZT1h bGGVydCZidG1fbWVkaXVtPWVtYWlsJnV0bV9jYW1wYWlnbbj13c F9uZXdzX2FsZXJ0X3JldmVyZSZsb2NhdGlvbj1hbGGVydCJ9. mIoiEPPltobXaqoitT1jJQBnniYRwbNxU8CwMsu4yw4&utm_c ampaign=wp_news_alert_revere&utm_medium=email&utm_ source=alert&wpisrc=al_news__alert-economy--alert-politics-- alert-national&wpmk=1.

34 Scheiber, N., & Conger, K. (February 18, 2020). The great Google Re- volt. *The New York Times Magazine.* Downloaded from: https://www. nytimes.com/interactive/2020/02/18/magazine/google-revolt.html.

35 Room, T., Darwell, D., Dwoskin, E., & Timberg, C. (April 10, 2020). Apple, Google debut major effort to help people track if they've come in contact with coronavirus. *The Washington Post.* Downloaded from: https://www. washingtonpost.com/technology/2020/04/10/apple-google-tracking- coronavirus/?utm_campaign=wp_news_alert_revere&utm_ medium=email&utm_source=alert&wpisrc=al_business__ alert-economy&wpmk=1.

36 MacMillan, D., Whoriskey, P., & O'Connell, J. (December 16, 2021). America's biggest companies are flourishing during the pandemic and putting thousands of people out of work. Downloaded from: https://www.washingtonpost.com/graphics/2020/business/ 50-biggest-companies-coronavirus-layoffs/.

37 Bright, J. (March 12, 2020). Covid-19 market turmoil tests NYSE's shutdown circuit-breakers. *Techcrunch.* Downloaded from: https:// techcrunch.com/2020/03/12/covid-19-market-turmoil-tests-nyses- shutdown-circuit-breakers/.

38 Korosec, K. (March 16, 2020). All major indices take a hit as Covid-19 pandemic continues. *Techcrunch.* Downloaded from: https:// techcrunch.com/2020/03/16/all-major-indices-take-a-hit-as-covid- 19-pandemic-continues/.

12 Building your strength

I hope you found *Exercising Your Ethics: Bringing Moral Strength to Business* innovative, fresh, and evocative, treating a philosophical topic in a straightforward manner. The chapters revealed the ironies and hypocrisies embedded within human behavior. Perhaps the examples highlighted ways in which you can improve and become more consistent with the values and principles you care about. It's good to recognize and find a bit of humor in our own incongruencies. Overall, however, the serious nature of ethics has made it abundantly clear that the responsibility for its presence in business resides within all of us.

Moral strength is an inside job. Do your part.

Given the daily grind and race to achieve quarterly profits, combined with a self-indulgent consumption-based economy, business has and will continue to shape our lives in ways that can threaten to degrade sustainability.

DOI: 10.4324/9780429324284-13

With your help, we can reverse this trend.

Feelings of fear, worry, and distrust experienced around the world, as a result of the pandemic, were combined with an ardent plea for social justice and racial equality in 2020. Business, government, and citizens are now called to work together to address public health and to resolve deeply entrenched societal ills. We witnessed some companies respond to these challenges with moral strength.

Find your role models. Be a role model.

As leaders, managers, employees, and citizens, we must learn to sustain, deliver, and nurture our compassion, mindfulness, empathy, patience, and kindness. This means we share in the responsibility to ensure our physical, mental, and spiritual health and well-being.

Rising above the worst within us and becoming our best selves is an ongoing effort. Virtues must be made authentic through meaningful, real, and lasting response-actions. Any challenge you find yourself in will benefit from the application of the skills you have read about in this book. The use of emotional signaling, pausing to reflect, self-regulation, and moral reinforcement can be applied in any situation to help you form a more thoughtful response-action.

Business has the power to cast harms into the future for generations to come. It can also be the lever for deep and lasting positive transformation. Every shareholder, stakeholder, and organizational member has the ability to help corporations move in a responsible direction. Let the strengths, emanating from each chapter in this book, help light the way forward.

Strength #1: "Business" and "ethics" are words that belong together. For a successful union, they must genuinely serve one another.

Strength #2: Being ethical is an investment in your own well-being, as you build a healthier workplace and society.

Strength #3: Expect and demand more from every corporation you do business with.

Strength #4: Ethical habits are shaped by your environment, including who you work with and for.

Strength #5: If the rules are not working to ensure ethical behavior, get involved to help change them.

Strength #6: Make decisions with the knowledge that all life is precious, more important than profits.

Strength #7: If you value honesty, quit lying.

Strength #8: Trust is a valuable commodity and the basis of lasting relationships in business.

Strength #9: Learn from your past to build a more ethical future.

Strength #10: To protect your moral identity, give it a workout!

Strength #11: Seek out help, until you have it.

The identified strengths will support your ability to effectively live the values you say you hold. By practicing the moral competencies, you will fortify ethics in your workplace. My sincere hope is that you benefit from a feeling of pride, as you exercise your ethics and bring moral strength to business.

Strength #12: Sustained efforts to be an ethical person will foster a sense of fulfillment and appreciation throughout a lifetime.

Gratitude

Life's a team sport

Like most everything in life, *Exercising Your Ethics* was a team effort. Ralph and I extend our appreciation to Lucy Sekerka, Bill Jenkins, Fiona Underhill, Trish Conklin, Anne Jenkins, Kathleen Kosiec, Lisa Villarreal, Marilyn MacLellan, Maryanne Neuwirth, and Dana Tomasino. Their feedback, comments, and editorial suggestions provided welcomed contributions. We also thank our proposal reviewers and the Routledge editorial staff for their interest in this project. Finally, we are deeply grateful to our generous *Ethics in Action Center* sponsors. Without their support, this book would not have been possible. Gratitude abounds!

DOI: 10.4324/9780429324284-14

Printed in Great Britain
by Amazon

76657971R00228